P9-CEV-957

SPIRITUAL   AUTHORITY

Spiritual Authority

WATCHMAN NEE

Christian Fellowship Publishers, Inc.
New York

Copyright © 1972
Christian Fellowship Publishers, Inc.
New York
All Rights Reserved

ISBN 0-935008-35-7

Available from the Publishers at:
11515 Allecingie Parkway
Richmond, Virginia 23235

PRINTED IN U.S.A.

CONTENTS

The contents of this volume comprise a series of messages which were delivered in Chinese by the author during a training period for workers held in Kuling, Foochow, China, in 1948, and are now translated from the edited notes taken by some who attended that training.

Scripture quotations are from the American Standard Version of the Bible (1901), unless otherwise indicated.

PART ONE

AUTHORITY AND SUBJECTION

1 | The Importance of Authority

Let every soul be in subjection to the higher powers: for there is no power but of God; and the powers that be are ordained of God. Therefore he that resisteth the power, withstandeth the ordinance of God: and they that withstand shall receive to themselves judgment. For rulers are not a terror to the good work, but to the evil. And wouldest thou have no fear of the power? do that which is good, and thou shalt have praise from the same: for he is a minister of God to thee for good. But if thou do that which is evil, be afraid; for he beareth not the sword in vain: for he is a minister of God, an avenger for wrath to him that doeth evil. Wherefore ye must needs be in subjection, not only because of the wrath, but also for conscience' sake. For for this cause ye pay tribute also; for they are ministers of God's service, attending continually upon this very thing. Render to all their dues: tribute to whom tribute is due; custom to whom custom; fear to whom fear; honor to whom honor. (Rom. 13.1-7)

Who being the effulgence of his glory, and the very image of his substance, and upholding all things by the word of his power, when he had made purification of sins, sat down on the right hand of the Majesty on high. (Heb. 1.3)

How art thou fallen from heaven, Lucifer, son of the morning! Thou art cut down to the ground, that didst prostrate the nations! And thou that didst say in thy heart, I will ascend into the heavens, I will exalt my throne above the stars of God, and I will sit upon the mount of assembly, in the recesses of the north; I will ascend above the heights of the clouds, I will be like the Most High. (Is. 14.12-14 Darby)

And bring us not into temptation, but deliver us from the evil one. (Matt. 6.13)

And the high priest stood up, and said unto him, Answerest thou nothing? what is it which these witness against thee? But Jesus held his peace. And the high priest said unto him, I adjure thee by the living God, that thou tell us whether thou art the Christ, the Son of God. Jesus saith unto him, Thou hast said: nevertheless I say unto you, Henceforth ye shall see the Son of man sitting at the right hand of Power, and coming on the clouds of heaven. (Matt. 26.62-64)

God's Throne Established on Authority

The acts of God issue from His throne, and His throne is established on His authority. All things are created through God's authority and all physical laws of the universe are maintained by His authority. Hence the Bible expresses it as "upholding all things by the word of his power," which means upholding all things by the word of the power of His authority. For God's authority represents God Himself whereas His power stands only for His act. Sin against power is more easily forgiven than sin against authority, because the latter is a sin against God Himself. God alone is authority in all things; all the authorities of the earth are instituted by God. Authority is a tremendous thing in the universe—nothing overshadows it. It is therefore imperative for us who desire to serve God to know the authority of God.

The Origin of Satan

The archangel turned into Satan when he overreached God's authority, competed with God, and thus became an adversary of

God. Rebellion was the cause of Satan's fall.

Both Isaiah 14.12-15 and Ezekiel 28.13-17 speak of the rise and fall of Satan. The first passage, though, lays stress on how Satan violated God's authority while the second passage emphasizes his trespassing against God's holiness. To offend God's authority is a rebellion far more serious than that of offending God's holiness. Since it is a matter of conduct, sinning is more easily forgiven than rebellion, the latter being a matter of principle. Satan's intent of setting his throne above the throne of God was the thing which violated God's authority; it was the principle of self-exaltation. The act of sinning was not the cause of Satan's fall; that act was but the product of his rebellion against authority. It was rebellion which God condemned.

In serving God we must not violate authorities, because to do so is a principle of Satan. How can we preach Christ according to Satan's principle? Yet it is possible in our work to stand with Christ in doctrine while at the same time stand with Satan in principle. How very wicked for us to assume that we are doing the work of the Lord. Please take note that Satan is not afraid of our preaching the word of Christ, yet how very much he is in fear of our being subject to the authority of Christ. Never should we who serve God serve according to the principle of Satan. Whenever the principle according to Christ is operating, that of Satan fades away. Satan is still a usurper today; he will be cast down at the time of the end of the book of Revelation. If we would truly serve God we must be completely purified from the principle of Satan.

In the prayer which our Lord teaches His church, the word "And bring us not into temptation" points to Satan's work, whereas the word "but deliver us from the evil one" refers directly to Satan himself. Immediately after these words the Lord makes a most significant declaration: "For thine is the kingdom, and the power, and the glory, for ever. Amen." (Matt. 6.13 margin) All kingdom, authority, and glory belong to God and to God alone. What sets us totally free from Satan is the seeing of this most precious truth—that the kingdom is God's.

Since the whole universe is under the dominion of God, we have to subject ourselves to His authority. Let no one steal God's glory.

Satan showed all the kingdoms of the earth to the Lord, but the Lord answered that the kingdom of the heavens is God's. We must see who it is who has the authority. We preach the gospel in order to bring men into God's authority, but how can we establish God's authority on earth if we ourselves have not met authority? How can we possibly deal with Satan?

Authority, the Controversy of the Universe

The controversy of the universe is centered on who shall have the authority, and our conflict with Satan is the direct result of our attributing authority to God. To maintain God's authority we must be subject to it with all our hearts. It is absolutely necessary for us to meet God's authority and to possess a basic knowledge of what it is.

Before he knew authority Paul tried to wipe out the church; after he had met the Lord on the Damascus road he saw that it was hard for the feet (human power) to kick against the goads (God's authority). He immediately fell to the ground and acknowledged Jesus as Lord. After that, he was able to submit to the directions given him by Ananias in the city of Damascus, for Paul had met God's authority. At the moment he was saved he knew God's authority as well as God's salvation.

How could Paul, being a clever and capable person, listen to the words of Ananias—an unknown little brother mentioned only once in the Bible—if he had not met the authority of God? Had he not encountered authority on the road to Damascus he could never have been subject to that obscure little brother in the city. This shows us that whoever has met authority deals purely with authority and not with man. Let us not see the man but only the authority vested in him. We do not obey man but God's authority in that man. Otherwise, how can we ever learn what authority is? We are on the wrong road if we meet man first before we obey authority. The opposite is the right way. Then we will not mind who the man is.

God has purposed to manifest His authority to the world through the church. God's authority can be seen in the coordination of the various members of the body of Christ.

God uses His utmost power to maintain His authority; therefore His authority is the hardest thing to come up against. We who are so self-righteous and yet so blind need once in our life to encounter God's authority so that we may be broken unto submission and so begin to learn obedience to the authority of God. Before a man can subject himself to God's delegated authority he must first meet God's inherent authority.

Obedience to God's Will—the Greatest Demand of the Bible

The greatest of God's demands on man is not for him to bear the cross, to serve, make offerings, or deny himself. The greatest demand is for him to obey. God ordered Saul to attack the Amalekites and destroy them utterly (1 Sam. 15). Yet after his victory Saul spared Agag, king of the Amalekites, along with the best of the sheep and oxen and the fatted beasts and lambs and all that was good. Saul would not devote them to destruction; he argued that these were spared to sacrifice to God. But Samuel said to him: "Behold, obedience is better than sacrifice, Attention than the fat of rams" (verse 15.22 Darby). The sacrifices mentioned here were sweet-savor offerings—having nothing to do with sin, for sin-offering was never called an offering of sweet-savor. They were offered for God's acceptance and satisfaction. Why did Samuel say that "obedience is better than sacrifice"? Because even in sacrifice there can be the element of self-will. Obedience alone is absolutely honoring to God, for it alone takes God's will as its center.

For authority to be expressed there must be subjection. If there is to be subjection, self needs to be excluded; but according to one's self-life, subjection is not possible. This is only possible when one lives in the Spirit. It is the highest expression of God's will.

Our Lord's Prayer in Gethsemane

Some think our Lord's prayer in Gethsemane when His sweat fell like great drops of blood was due to the weakness of His flesh, to His fear of drinking the cup. Not at all, for the prayer in Gethsemane is on the same principle as 1 Samuel 15.22. It is the highest prayer in which our Lord expresses His obedience to God's authority. Our Lord obeys God's authority first, more than sacrificing Himself on the cross. He prays earnestly that He may know what is the will of God. He does not say, "I want to be crucified, I must drink the cup." He merely insists on obeying. He says in effect, "If it be possible for me not to go to the cross," but even here He has not His own will. Immediately He continues with, "but Thy will be done."

The will of God is the absolute thing; the cup (that is, the crucifixion) is not absolute. Should God will it that the Lord not be crucified, then He would not need to go to the cross. Before He knew the will of God, the cup and God's will were two separate things; after He knew it was of God, however, the cup and God's will merged into one. Will represents authority. Therefore, to know God's will and to obey it is to be subject to authority. But how can one be subject to authority if he does not pray or have the heart to know God's will?

"The cup which the Father hath given me, shall I not drink it?" says the Lord (John 18.11). Here He maintains the supremacy of the authority of God, not of His cross. Further, having once understood that drinking the cup—that is, being crucified for atonement—is God's will, He instantly says: "Arise, let us be going" (Matt. 26.46). In going to the cross He accomplishes God's will. Consequently the Lord's death is the highest expression of obedience to authority. Even the cross, the crux of the universe, cannot be higher than God's will. The Lord maintains God's authority (the will of God) more than His own cross (His sacrifice).

To serve God we are not called to choose self-denial or sacrifice, rather are we called to fulfill God's purpose. The basic principle is not to choose the cross but to obey God's will. Should the principle on which we work and serve include rebellion, then Satan will obtain and enjoy glory even through our sacrifices. Saul might offer sheep and oxen, yet God never accepted them as sacrifices to Himself because there was a Satanic principle involved. To overthrow God's authority is to overthrow God. That is why the Scripture indicates that "rebellion is as the sin of divination, and selfwill is as iniquity and idolatry" (1 Sam. 15.23 Darby).

As God's servants, the first thing we should meet is authority. To touch authority is as practical as touching salvation, but it is a deeper lesson. Before we can work for God we must be overturned by His authority. Our entire relationship with God is regulated by whether or not we have met authority. If we have, then we shall encounter authority everywhere, and being thus restrained by God we can begin to be used by Him.

How Our Lord and Paul Acted under Judgment

Matthew 26 records the two-fold judgment which our Lord Jesus underwent following his arrest. Before the high priest He received religious judgment and before Pilate, political judgment. When He was judged by Pilate the Lord made no answer, for He was not under earthly jurisdiction. But when the high priest adjured Him by the living God, then He replied. This is obedience to authority. Again, as recorded in Acts 23, when Paul was being judged he quickly submitted, upon discovering that Ananias was the high priest of God.

Hence we who labor must be brought face to face with authority. Otherwise our work will be under the rebellious principle of Satan and we will work without the need of knowing

God's will. We will not be under the principle of obedience to authority. Yet it is only by working under obedience to authority that we can work in accordance with the will of God. Oh, this truly requires a great revelation!

In Matthew 7.21-23 we find our Lord reprimanding those who prophesy and cast out demons and do many mighty things in His name. Why are they disapproved? Because they make self their starting point; they themselves do things in the name of the Lord. This is the activity of the flesh. Wherefore our Lord pronounces them to be evildoers instead of His laborers. He emphasizes that only that person who does the will of His Father shall enter the kingdom of the heavens. This alone is work in obedience to God's will, that which originates with God. We are not to find work to do, rather are we to be sent to work by God. Once having understood this we shall truly experience the reality of the authority of the kingdom of the heavens.

To See Authority Requires a Great Revelation

There are two important matters in the universe: trusting in God's salvation and obeying His authority. Trust and obey. The Bible defines sin as lawlessness (1 John 3.4). The word in Romans 2.12 "without" law is the same as "against" law. Lawlessness is disobeying God's authority; and this is sin. Sinning is a matter of conduct but lawlessness is a matter of heart attitude. This present age is characterized by lawlessness. The world is full of the sin of lawlessness, and soon the son of lawlessness shall appear. Authority in the world is being increasingly undermined until at the end all authorities will be overthrown and lawlessness shall rule.

Let us know that there are two principles in the universe: the principle of God's authority and the principle of Satanic rebellion. We cannot serve God and simultaneously go the way of rebellion by having a rebellious spirit. Satan laughs when a rebellious person preaches the word, for in that person is dwelling the satanic principle. The principle of service must be authority. Are we going to obey God's authority or not? We who serve God must have this basic understanding of authority. Anyone who has once experienced an electric shock knows thereafter that he cannot be careless with electricity. Likewise, a person who has once been smitten by God's authority from then on has his eyes opened to judge what is lawless both in himself and in others.

May God be gracious to us by delivering us from rebellion. Only after we have known God's authority and learned obedience can we lead His children in the straight path.

2 | Old Testament Instances of Rebellion

1. THE FALL OF ADAM AND EVE.

And Jehovah God commanded the man, saying, Of every tree of the garden thou mayest freely eat: but of the tree of the knowledge of good and evil, thou shalt not eat of it: for in the day that thou eatest thereof thou shalt surely die. (Gen. 2.16-17)

Now the serpent was more subtle than any beast of the field which Jehovah God had made. And he said unto the woman, Yea, hath God said, Ye shall not eat of any tree of the garden? And the woman said unto the serpent, Of the fruit of the trees of the garden we may eat; but of the fruit of the tree which is in the midst of the garden, God hath said, Ye shall not eat of it, neither shall ye touch it, lest ye die. And the serpent said unto the woman, Ye shall not surely die: for God doth know that in the day ye eat thereof, then your eyes shall be opened, and ye shall be as God, knowing good and evil. And when the woman saw that the tree was good for food, and that it was a delight to the eyes, and that the tree was to be desired to make one wise, she took of the fruit thereof, and did eat; and she gave also unto her husband with her, and he did eat. (Gen. 3.1-6)

For as through the one man's disobedience the many were made sinners. (Rom. 5.19)

Man's Fall Due to Disobedience

Let us review the story of Adam and Eve as recorded in

Genesis Chapters 2 and 3. After God had created Adam, He gave him a few charges; among these was the order to not eat the fruit of the tree of the knowledge of good and evil. The crux of this charge was more than the forbiddance to eat a certain fruit; rather was it that God was putting Adam under authority that he might learn obedience. On the one hand God placed all the created things on the earth under the authority of Adam that he might have dominion over them; but on the other hand God placed Adam himself under *His* authority that Adam might obey authority. Only the one who is under authority can be an authority.

According to the order of God's creation God made Adam before He made Eve. He put Adam in authority and Eve under Adam's authority. He set these two: the one as the authority and the other to be in subjection. In both the old and the new creation this order of priority is the basis of authority. Whoever is first created is to be the authority; whoever is first saved is to be the authority. Therefore, wherever we go, our first thought must be to find out who are those to whom God wants us to be subject. We can find authority everywhere and learn to obey authority at anytime.

The fall of man is due to disobedience to God's authority. Instead of obeying Adam, Eve made her own decision upon seeing that the fruit was good and pleasant to the eyes. She uncovered her head. Her eating the fruit did not come out of subjection but out of her own will. She not only violated God's order but disobeyed Adam as well. To rebel against God's representative authority is the same as to rebel against God. In listening to Eve and eating the forbidden fruit Adam sinned against God's direct will; hence he too was disobedient to God's authority. This also was rebellion.

All Work Must Be Done in Obedience

Eve was put not only under God's authority but also, in

God's ordering, under Adam's authority. She had a double authority to obey. And our position today is no different from this. Now Eve, seeing that it was good for food, ate the fruit without inquiring as to whom she was obeying. Yet from the very beginning God had ordered man to obey and not to be self-willed. Eve's action, however, was not governed by obedience; it was initiated by her own will. She was not subject to God's order nor did she obey God's authority. She instead made up her own mind. She rebelled against God and fell. Any action which lacks in obedience is a fall, and any act of disobedience is rebellion.

As man's obedience increases, his actions decrease. When we first begin to follow the Lord we are full of activity but quite short on obedience. But as we advance in spirituality our actions gradually diminish until we are filled with obedience. Many, however, do what they like and refuse to do what they dislike. They never ponder whether or not they are acting out of obedience. Hence many works are done out of self and not in obedience to God.

Right or Wrong Is in God's Hand

Man's action should not be governed by the knowledge of good or evil; it should be motivated by a sense of obedience. The principle of good and evil is to live according to what is right or what is wrong. Before Adam and Eve ate the forbidden fruit their right and wrong were in God's hand. If they did not live before God they knew nothing at all, for their right and wrong actually were in God. By taking the fruit of the tree of the knowledge of good and evil, they found a source of right and wrong in other than God Himself. Consequently, after the fall men need not find in God the sense of right and wrong. They have it in themselves. This is the result of the fall. The work of redemption is to bring us back to the place where we will now find our right and wrong in God.

Christians Should Obey Authority

There is no authority except from God; all authorities have been instituted by Him. By tracing all authorities back to their source we invariably end up with God. God is above all authorities, and all authorities are under Him. In touching God's authority we touch God Himself. God's work basically is done not by power but by authority. He upholds all things by the powerful word of His authority, even as He created them by the same word. His word of command is authority. We cannot say how God's authority works; nevertheless, we know that He accomplishes everything by it.

A beloved servant of a centurion was sick. The centurion knew he was both under authority and in authority over others. So he asked the Lord to but say a word, believing the work of healing would thus be done—for are not all authorities in the Lord's hand? He believed in the Lord's authority. No wonder our Lord commended him for his great faith: "Verily I say unto you, I have not found so great faith, no, not in Israel" (Matt. 8.10). Touching God's authority is the same as meeting God. Today the universe is full of authorities set up by God. All the laws of the universe are established by God. Everything is under His authority. Whenever a person sins against God's authority he sins against God. All Christians must therefore learn to obey authority.

First Lesson a Worker Should Learn Is Obey Authority

We are under men's authority as well as having men under our authority. This is our position. Even the Lord Jesus on earth was subject not only to God but also to other's authority. Authority is everywhere. There is authority in the school, authority in the home. The policeman on the street, though perhaps less learned than you, is set up by God as your authority. Whenever a few brothers in Christ come together, immediately a spiritual order falls into place. A Christian worker ought to know who is above him. Some do not know who are the authorities above them, hence they do not obey. We should not be occupied with right or wrong, good or evil; rather should we know who is the authority above us. Once we learn to whom we must be subject, we naturally find our place in the body. Alas, how many Christians today have not the faintest idea concerning subjection. No wonder there is so much confusion and disorder. For this reason, obedience to authority is the first lesson a worker ought to learn; and it also occupies a large place in the work itself.

Obedience Must Be Recovered

Since the fall of Adam disorder has prevailed in the universe. Everyone thinks he is able to distinguish good from evil and to judge what is right or wrong. He seems to know better than God. This is the folly of the fall. We need to be delivered from such a deception, because this is nothing other than rebellion.

Our knowledge of obedience is woefully inadequate. Some seem to think their obedience is complete and full upon their obedience to the Lord in baptism. Many young students look upon God's command to obey their teachers as harsh treatment. Many wives consider the divine command of being subject to difficult husbands as quite cruel. Countless Christians are living today in a state of rebellion; they have not so much as learned the first lesson in obedience.

The subjection taught in the Bible is concerned with being subject to the authorities established by God. How superficial was the old presentation of obedience! Obedience is a foundational principle. If this matter of authority remains unsolved, nothing can be solved. As faith is the principle by which we obtain life, so obedience is the principle by which that life is lived out. The divisions and disruptions currently within the church stem from rebellion. In order to recover authority, obedience must first be restored. Many have cultivated the habit of being the head, yet without ever having known obedience. We must therefore learn a lesson. Let obedience be our first reaction. God has not withheld anything from us concerning authority. He has already shown us how to be subject to both direct and indirect authority. Many profess they know how to obey God, but they really know nothing as to obeying delegated authority. Since all authorities come from God we must learn to obey them all. The problems facing us in our day are due to men living outside the authority of God.

No Unity of Body Without Authority of Head

God is working towards recovering the oneness of the body. But for this to be accomplished there must first be the life of the Head, followed next by the authority of the Head. Without the life of the Head there can be no body. Without the authority of the Head there can be no unity of the body. To maintain the oneness of the body we must let the life of the Head rule.

God wishes us to obey His delegated authorities as well as Himself. All the members of the body should be subject to one another. When this is so, the body is one with itself and with the Head. As the authority of the Head prevails, the will of God is done. Thus does the church become the kingdom of God.

Some Lessons on Obedience

Sooner or later, those who serve God must meet authority in the universe, in society, in the home, in the church. How can one serve and obey God if he has never met the authority of God? This is more than a matter of teaching or doctrine, for a teaching can be abstract. Some think it is very difficult to know how to obey authority, but if we have met God the difficulty evaporates. There is no one who can obey God's authority without God's mercy being upon him. Let us therefore learn a few lessons:

1. Have a spirit of obedience.

2. Practice obedience. Some individuals are like savages who just cannot obey. But those who are trained do not feel bound no matter where they are placed. They can naturally live out obedience.

3. Learn to exercise delegated authority. He who works for God needs not only to learn to obey authority but also to learn how to be God's delegated authority in the church and in the home. Once you have learned how to be under God's authority, you will count yourself as nothing even after God entrusts you with much.

Some learn only obedience, and fail to know how to be in authority when they are sent to some place to work. It is necessary to learn how both to be under authority and in authority. The church suffers from many who do not know how to obey, but she is likewise damaged through some who have not learned how to be in authority.

2. THE REBELLION OF HAM.

> And Noah began to be a husbandman, and planted a vineyard: and he drank of the wine and was drunken; and he was uncovered within his tent. And Ham, the father of Canaan, saw the nakedness of his father, and told his two brethren without. And Shem and Japheth took a garment, and laid it upon both their shoulders, and went backward, and covered the nakedness of their father; and their faces were backward, and they saw not their father's nakedness. And Noah awoke from his wine, and knew what his youngest son had done unto him. And he said, Cursed be Canaan; A servant of servants shall he be unto his brethren. And he said, Blessed be Jehovah, the God of Shem; And let Canaan be his servant. God enlarge Japheth, and let him dwell in the tents of Shem; and let Canaan be his servant. (Gen. 9.20-27)

Failure of Delegated Authority Tests Obedience

In the Garden of Eden, Adam fell. In the vineyard, Noah also was defeated, but because of his righteousness God saved the family of Noah. In God's plan Noah was the head of the family. God put the whole family under Noah's authority; He also set Noah as the head of the world of that time.

But one day Noah became drunk in his vineyard and he uncovered himself in his tent. His youngest son, Ham, saw his father's nakedness and told his two brothers outside. So far as Noah's conduct was concerned, he certainly was wrong; he should not have been drunk. Yet Ham failed to see the dignity of authority. The father is God's instituted authority in the home, but the flesh delights in seeing a defect in authority so as to throw off all restraint. When Ham saw his father's improper conduct he did not have the slightest sense of shame or sorrow, nor did he try to cover his father's fault. This reveals that he had a rebellious spirit. He went out instead and told his brethren, pointing out to them his father's ugliness and so adding to himself the sin of reviling. Observe, though, how Shem and Japheth managed the situation. They entered the tent backwards—thus avoiding seeing their father's nakedness—and covered their father with the upper garment which they had laid on their shoulders.

It is seen then that the failure of Noah became a test to Shem, Ham, Japheth, and Ham's son, Canaan. It revealed who was obedient and who was rebellious. Noah's fall unveiled Ham's rebellion.

After Noah awoke from the wine he prophesied that the descendants of Ham would be cursed and would become the slaves of slaves to their brethren. The first one in the Bible to become a slave was Ham. Thrice was the sentence pronounced that Canaan would be a slave. This is to say that the one who is not subject to authority shall be slave to him who does obey authority. Shem was to be blessed. Even our Lord Jesus came from Shem. Japheth was destined to preach Christ, and thus it is that the nations that propagate the gospel today belong to the descendants of Japheth. The first to be cursed after the flood was Ham. Not knowing authority, he was put under authority for generations to follow. Everyone who wishes to serve the Lord needs to meet authority. No one can serve in the spirit of lawlessness.

3. STRANGE FIRE OFFERED BY NADAB AND ABIHU.

And Nadab and Abihu, the sons of Aaron, took each of

them his censer, and put fire therein, and laid incense theron, and offered strange fire before Jehovah, which he had not commanded them. And there came forth fire from before Jehovah, and devoured them, and they died before Jehovah. (Lev. 10.1-2)

Why Nadab and Abihu Were Burned

How sobering is the story of Nadab and Abihu! They served as priests, yet not because they were personally right but because they belonged to the family which God had chosen. God had set Aaron to be priest and the anointing oil was poured upon his head. In all matters of service Aaron was the chief; his sons were mere helpers, serving beside the altar in obedience to Aaron. God never meant to let the sons of Aaron serve independently; He placed them under the authority of Aaron. Twelve times Aaron and his sons are mentioned in Leviticus 8. In the next chapter Aaron offered sacrifices, with his sons helping him at his side. If Aaron made no move, his sons also ought not to move. Everything began with Aaron, not with his sons. Were the sons to venture to offer sacrifices by themselves, they would be offering strange fire. This, however, was exactly what Nadab and Abihu, the sons of Aaron, did. They thought they could offer sacrifices by themselves and so they offered without Aaron's order. The meaning of strange fire is to serve without an order, to serve without obedience to authority. They had watched their father offer; to them it was rather simple. And so they assumed that they could do the same thing. Nadab and Abihu only thought of whether or not they were able to do the same. They failed to see who represented God's authority.

Service Is Initiated by God

Here we face a most serious problem: serving God and offering strange fire seem to be very much alike, and yet they are worlds apart. True service is initiated by God. When man serves under God's authority, he is thereby accepted. Strange fire originates from man. It does not require knowing the will of God or obeying the authority of God. It is wholly done through man's own zeal, and it ends up in death. If it happens that our service and work become increasingly dead, it is time for us to ask for God's enlightenment as to whether we are serving in the true principle of service or according to the principle of strange fire.

God's Work Is the Coordination of Authority

Nadab and Abihu worked apart from Aaron; hence they worked independently of God. The work of God must be coordinated under authority: God wanted Nadab and Abihu to serve under Aaron's authority. Notice in the New Testament how Barnabas and Paul, Paul and Timothy, and Peter and Mark worked together. Some were responsible while others were helping. In God's work He sets some to be in authority with others to be under authority. God has called us to be priests after the order of Melchizedek; we must therefore serve God according to the order of coordinated authority.

He who inordinately lifts his head and acts independently is being rebellious, the consequence of which is death. Whoever tries to serve without first meeting authority is offering strange fire. Anyone who says "If *he* can, *I* can too" is in a state of rebellion. God is not only careful to see that there is fire, He is also keen to notice the nature of the fire. Rebellion changes the nature of a fire. That which was not ordered by Jehovah nor by Aaron was strange fire. What God looks for is not the matter of sacrifice but the question of maintaining authority. Consequently men ought to learn how to follow, how to forever occupy a minor role.

Just as the delegated authority follows God, so those who are subject to authority should follow God's delegated authority. There is no place for isolated individual service. In spiritual work all must serve in coordination. Coordination is the rule; the individual is not the unit. Nadab and Abihu were out of coordination with Aaron, hence they were out of coordination with God. They should not have left Aaron and served independently. Those who violated authority would be consumed by fire from before God. And though Aaron was not conscious of the seriousness of this matter, Moses realized how serious it was to rebel against God's authority. Today many are trying to serve God independently. They have never been under authority; they unwittingly sin against God's authority.

4. THE REVILING OF AARON AND MIRIAM.

And Miriam and Aaron spake against Moses because of the Cushite woman whom he had married; for he had married a Cushite woman. And they said, Hath Jehovah indeed spoken only with Moses? Hath he not spoken also with us? And Jehovah heard it. Now the man Moses was very meek, above all the men that were upon the face of the earth.

And Jehovah spake suddenly unto Moses, and unto Aaron, and unto Miriam, Come out ye three unto the tent of meeting. And the three came out. And Jehovah came down in a pillar of cloud, and stood at the door of the tent, and called Aaron and Miriam; and they both came forth. And he said, Hear now my words: if there be a prophet among you, I Jehovah will make myself known unto him in a vision, I will speak with him in a dream. My servant Moses is not so; he is faithful in all my house: with him will I speak mouth to mouth, even manifestly, and not in dark speeches; and the form of Jehovah shall he behold; wherefore then were ye not afraid to speak against my servant, against Moses?

And the anger of Jehovah was kindled against them; and he departed. And the cloud removed from over the Tent; and, behold, Miriam was leprous, as white as snow: and Aaron looked upon Miriam, and behold, she was leprous. And Aaron said unto Moses, Oh, my lord, lay not, I pray thee, sin upon us, for that we have done foolishly, and for that we have sinned. Let her not, I pray, be as one dead, of whom the flesh is half consumed when he cometh out of his mother's womb. And Moses cried unto Jehovah, saying, Heal her, O God, I beseech thee. And Jehovah said unto Moses, If her father had but spit in her face, should she not be ashamed seven days? let her be shut up without the camp seven days, and after that she shall be brought in again. And Miriam was shut up without the camp seven days: and the people journeyed not till Miriam was brought in again. (Num. 12)

To Speak Against Representative Authority Incurs Divine Wrath

Aaron and Miriam were elder brother and sister to Moses. Thus in the home Moses should be subject to their authority. But in the calling and work of God they ought to subject themselves to Moses' authority. They were not happy with the Ethiopian woman whom Moses had married, so they spoke against Moses by saying, "Hath Jehovah indeed spoken only with Moses? hath he not spoken also with us?" An Ethiopian is an African, a descendant of Ham. Moses should not have married this Ethiopian woman. As an older sister, Miriam could reprimand her brother on the basis of their family relationship. But when she opened her mouth to slander she touched upon the work of God, challenging the position of Moses.

God had entrusted His delegated authority in the work to Moses. How wrong it was for Aaron and Miriam to attack Moses' position on the basis of a family reason. It was God who had chosen Moses to lead the people of Israel out of Egypt, nevertheless Miriam despised Moses. For this God was greatly displeased with her. She could deal with her brother, but she could not revile God's authority. The trouble was that neither Aaron nor Miriam recognized God's authority. In standing on natural ground they conceived a rebellious heart.

Yet Moses did not answer back. He knew that if he had been set up by God to be the authority he need not defend himself. Whoever reviled him touched death. So long as God gave him authority he could remain silent. A lion needs no protection, since full authority lies within it. Moses was able to represent God in authority because he had first been subject to God's authority, for he was very meek, above all men who were upon the face of the earth. The authority which Moses represented was God's own. And no one can take away God-given authority.

Rebellious words ascend to heaven and are heard by God. When Aaron and Miriam sinned against Moses, they sinned against God who was in Moses. The anger of the Lord was kindled against them. Whenever man touches God's delegated authority he touches God within that person; sinning against delegated authority is sinning against God.

Authority Is God's Choice, Not Man's Attainment

God summoned the three to the tent of meeting. Aaron and Miriam went without any hesitation, because they thought God must be on their side and also because they had much to say to God since Moses had caused all these troubles in the family by marrying an Ethiopian woman. But God proclaimed that Moses was His servant who was faithful in all His house. How dare they speak against His servant? Spiritual authority is not something one attains to by effort. It is given by God to whomever He chooses. How very different is the spiritual from the natural.

God Himself is the authority. Beware lest we offend. Whoever speaks against Moses speaks against God's chosen one. Let us never despise God's chosen vessel.

Rebellion Is Manifested in Leprosy

The anger of the Lord was kindled against them and the

cloud departed from off the tent. God's presence was lost, and immediately Miriam became leprous as snow. Her leprosy did not come through contamination; it was clearly a chastisement of God. To be leprous was in no way better than to be an Ethiopian woman. Miriam's inward rebellion was manifested in outward leprosy. And she who had thus become leprous must be isolated, losing all communication with others.

When Aaron saw that Miriam was leprous, he entreated Moses to act as mediator and pray for healing. God said, "If her father had but spit in her face, should she not be ashamed seven days? let her be shut up without the camp seven days, and after that she shall be brought in again." And as a result, the journey of the tent was delayed seven days. Whenever there is rebellion and reviling among us we shall lose the presence of God, and the earthly tent becomes immovable. God's pillar of cloud will not descend until those words of reviling have been dealt with. If this matter of authority is not solved all else becomes void and vain.

Besides Direct Authority, Be Subject to Representative Authority

Many consider themselves obedient to God while actually knowing nothing of being subject to God's delegated authority. He who is truly obedient will find God's authority in every circumstance, in the home, and in other institutions. God asked, "Why are you not afraid to revile against my servant?" Special attention must be paid each time words of reviling are uttered. Such words should not be idly spoken. Reviling proves that there is a rebellious spirit within; it is the germination of rebellion. We ought to fear God and not speak carelessly. But there are those today who speak against the elders in the church or others above them; they do not realize the gravity of their speaking so. When the church is revived in the grace of God, those who have reviled will be treated as leprous.

May God be gracious to us that we may understand that this is not a matter of our brother, but a matter of God's instituted authority. After we have met authority we will realize how much we have sinned against God. Our concept of sin will undergo a drastic change. We shall look at sin as God sees it. We will see that the sin which God condemns is the rebellion of man.

5. THE REBELLION OF KORAH, DATHAN, AND ABIRAM.

Collective Rebellion

An instance of collective rebellion is recorded in Chapter 16 of Numbers. Korah and his company belonged to the Levites; therefore they represented the spiritual ones. On the other hand, Dathan and Abiram were sons of Reuben, and so they stood for the leading ones. All these, together with two hundred and fifty leaders of the congregation, assembled to rebel against Moses and Aaron. They arbitrarily attacked the two saying, "Ye take too much upon you, seeing all the congregation are holy, every one of them, and Jehovah is among them: wherefore then lift ye up yourselves above the assembly of Jehovah?" (verse 3) They were disrespectful of Moses and Aaron. They may have been quite honest in what they said, yet they failed to see the authority of the Lord. They considered this matter a personal problem, as if there were no authority among God's people. In their attack they did not mention Moses' relationship with God nor the commandment of God.

Nevertheless, even under these serious accusations Moses neither got angry nor lost his temper. He simply fell on his face before the Lord. Since authority belongs to the Lord, he would not use any authority nor do anything for himself. He told Korah and his company to wait until the next morning when the Lord would show who was His and who was holy. Thus did he answer the wrong spirit with a right spirit.

What Korah and his party said was based on reason and conjecture; Moses, however, answered, "Jehovah will show who are his, and who is holy, and will cause him to come near unto him" (verse 5). The question was not with Moses, but with the Lord. The people thought they were merely opposing Moses and Aaron; they had not the slightest intention of being rebellious to God, for they still wished to serve Him. They were merely scornful of Moses and Aaron.

But, God and His delegated authority are inseparable. It is not possible to maintain one attitude towards God and another attitude towards Moses and Aaron. No one can reject God's delegated authority with one hand and receive God with the other hand. If they would submit themselves to the authority of Moses and Aaron they would then be in subjection to God.

Moses, however, did not lift himself up because of the authority God had given him. Instead, he humbled himself under the authority of God and answered his accuser with meekness, saying, "This do: take you censers, Korah, and all his company; and put fire in them and put incense upon them before Jehovah to-morrow: and it shall be that the man whom Jehovah doth choose, he shall be holy" (verses 6-7). Being more matured, he foresaw the consequence; so he sighed, "Ye take too much upon you, ye sons of Levi: . . . seemeth it but a small thing unto you, that the God of Israel hath separated you from the congregation of Israel, to bring you near to himself, to do the service of the tabernacle of Jehovah, and to stand before the congregation to minister unto them? . . . Therefore thou and all thy company are gathered together against Jehovah" (verses 7-11).

Dathan and Abiram were not present at the moment. For when Moses had sent to call them, they refused to come but grumbled, "Is it a small thing that thou hast brought us up out of a land flowing with milk and honey (Egypt), to kill us in the wilderness? wilt thou put out the eyes of these men?" (verses 13-14) Their attitude was most rebellious. They believed not in God's promise; what they looked for was earthly blessing. They forgot that it was through their own fault they did not enter Canaan; instead they spoke sharply against Moses.

God Wiped Rebellion Out of His People

At this juncture Moses' anger was aroused. Instead of speaking to them, he prayed to God. How frequently man's rebellion forces the judicial hand of God. Ten times the Israelites tempted God and five times they disbelieved Him, and God forbore and forgave; but for the rebellion of this time God came out to judge. Said God, "Let me consume the congregation in a moment" (see verse 21); He would wipe out rebellion from among His people. But Moses and Aaron fell on their faces and prayed, "Shall one man sin, and wilt thou be wroth with all the congregation?" (verse 22). God answered their prayer but judged Korah and his company. The authority whom God set up was the person to whom Israel must listen. Even God Himself testified before the Israelites that He too would accept the words of Moses.

Rebellion is a hellish principle. These people rebelled, and so the gate of Sheol was opened. The earth opened its mouth and swallowed up all the men who belonged to Korah, Dathan, and Abiram, and all their goods. Hence they and all which belonged to them went down alive into Sheol (verses 32-33). The gates of Hades shall not prevail against the church, but a rebellious spirit can open its gates. One reason the church sometimes does not prevail is because of the presence of the rebellious. The earth will not open its mouth unless there is a rebellious spirit. All sins release the power of death, but the sin of rebellion releases it the most. Only the obedient can shut Hades' gates and release life.

The Obedient Follow Faith, Not Reason

For the Israelites to complain that Moses had not brought them into a land flowing with milk and honey nor given them an inheritance of fields with vineyards was not without reason. They were still in the wilderness and had yet to enter the land of milk and honey. But please notice here; he who walks after reason and sight goes the way of reason; only he who obeys authority enters Canaan by faith. None who follow reason can walk the spiritual pathway, because it is beyond and above human reasoning. The faithful alone may enjoy spiritual abundance, those who by faith accept the pillar of cloud and of fire and the leadership of God's delegated authority such as that represented by Moses.

The earth opens its mouth to hasten the downfall of the disobedient into Sheol, for they are traveling in the way of death. The eyes of the disobedient are quite sharp but, alas, all they see is the barrenness of the wilderness. Though those who proceed by faith may appear to be blind, for they do not notice the barrenness before them, yet their eyes of faith see the better promise which lies ahead. And thus they enter Canaan. Therefore, men ought to be under the restraint of God's authority and learn to be led by God's delegated authority. Those who meet only fathers, brothers, and sisters do not know what authority is, and hence have not met God. In brief, then, authority is not a matter of outside instruction but of inward revelation.

Rebellion Is Contagious

There are *two* instances of rebellion in Numbers 16. From verse 1 to verse 40 the leaders rebelled; from verse 41 to verse 50 the whole congregation rebelled. The spirit of rebellion is very contagious. The judgment of the two hundred and fifty leaders who offered incense did not bring pause to the whole congregation. They were still rebellious, declaring that Moses had killed their leaders. But Moses and Aaron could not command the earth to open its mouth! It was God who so commanded. Moses could not call down fire to burn up the people! The fire came from the Lord God.

Human eyes see only men; they know not that authority comes from God. Such people are so bold that they do not fear, even though they have seen judgment. How dangerous is the lack of the knowledge of authority. When the whole congregation assembled against Moses and Aaron, the glory of the Lord appeared. This proved that the authority was of God. God came forth to execute judgment. A plague began, and fourteen thousand seven hundred people died by the plague. In the midst of this, Moses' spiritual sense was most keen; immediately he asked Aaron to take his censer and put fire therein from off the altar and lay incense in it and carry it quickly to the congregation and make atonement for them. And as Aaron stood between the dead and the living, the plague was stopped.

God could forbear their murmurings in the wilderness ten times, but He would not allow them to resist His authority. Many sins God can bear and forbear, but rebellion He cannot stand, because rebellion is the principle of death, the principle of Satan. Hence the sin of rebellion is more serious than any other sin. Whenever man resists authority, God immediately judges. How solemn this is!

4 | David's Knowledge of Authority

And the men of David said unto him, Behold, the day of which Jehovah said unto thee, Behold, I will deliver thine enemy into thy hand, and thou shalt do to him as it shall seem good unto thee. Then David arose, and cut off the skirt of Saul's robe privily. And it came to pass afterward, that David's heart smote him, because he had cut off Saul's skirt. And he said unto his men, Jehovah forbid that I should do this thing unto my lord, Jehovah's anointed, to put forth my hand against him, seeing he is Jehovah's anointed. (1 Sam. 24.4-6)

And David said to Abishai, Destroy him not; for who can put forth his hand against Jehovah's anointed, and be guiltless?. . .Jehovah forbid that I should put forth my hand against Jehovah's anointed. (1 Sam. 26.9,11)

And David said unto him, How wast thou not afraid to put forth thy hand to destroy Jehovah's anointed? (2 Sam. 1.14)

Not at Price of Rebellion Did David Seek the Throne

The time God formally inaugurated His authority on earth was at the time the kingdom of Israel was established. The Israelites, having entered Canaan, asked God for a king. Whereupon God commissioned Samuel to anoint Saul to be the first king. Saul was chosen and set up by God to be His delegated authority. Unfortunately, after he became king he disobeyed

God's authority even to the point of seeking to destroy it. He spared the king of the Amalekites and the best of the sheep, the oxen, the fatlings, and the lambs and all that was good. Since this was done in disobedience to God's word, God rejected Saul and anointed David. Nevertheless, David was still a man under Saul's authority. He was numbered among Saul's people, was enlisted in Saul's army, and was later chosen as Saul's son-in-law. Hence both of them were anointed. But then many times Saul sought to kill David. Israel now had two kings! The rejected one was still on the throne; the chosen one had not yet ascended David was in a most difficult position.

Saul went to seek David in the wilderness of Engedi. Along the way he entered a cave in which were sitting David and his men in the innermost part. The men of David suggested to him that he should kill Saul, but David resisted the temptation for he dared not raise his hand against authority. So far as the throne was concerned, was it not that David was anointed by God? And since he was standing directly in the plan and will of God, could anyone forbid him from being king? Why, then, should David not help himself to be king? Would it not be a good move to help God accomplish His will? Yet David strongly felt he could not kill Saul. To do so would be to rebel against God's authority, since the anointing of the Lord was still on Saul. Though Saul was rejected, he was nonetheless God's anointed—one set up by God. Were Saul to be killed at this moment, David could immediately ascend to the throne and the will of God need not be delayed for many years. But David was a man who knew how to deny himself. He would rather delay his own ascension than be a rebellious person. That is why he finally became God's delegated authority.

Once God had installed Saul as king and had put David under Saul's authority, David would have had to pay the price of rebellion to get to the throne by killing Saul. He would have had to become a rebel. This he dared not do. The principle involved is similar to Michael's restraint from pronouncing a reviling judgment upon Satan (Jude 9). Authority, we can therefore see, is a matter of extremely deep implications.

Obedience Higher Than Work

If men are to serve God subjection to authority is an absolute necessity. Obedience transcends our work. Should David rule his kingdom but fail to be subject to God's authority, he would be as useless as Saul. The same principle of rebellion works both in the Old Testament Saul and in the New Testament Judas: the first spared the best of the sheep and of the oxen, while the second coveted the thirty pieces of silver. Consecration does not cover the sin of rebellion. David did not dare kill Saul with his own hand in order to expedite God's plan and will. He waited for God to work; his heart was in quiet obedience. Even that one time when he cut off Saul's skirt, his heart smote him.

David's spiritual sense was as keen as that of New Testament believers. Today we should not merely condemn killing, even a smaller action such as the cutting off of another's skirt with a small knife is to be condemned, for it too is rebellion. Backbiting or bad manners or inward resistance may not be classified as killing, yet they certainly constitute the same as cutting off the skirt. They all originate from a rebellious spirit.

David was one who knew the authority of God in his heart. Although repeatedly chased by Saul, he submitted himself to God's authority. He even addressed Saul as "my lord" or "the Lord's anointed." This reveals an important fact: subjection to authority is not a being subject to a person, but a being subject to the anointing which is upon that person, the anointing which came to him when God ordained him to be an authority. David recognized the anointing upon Saul and acknowledged that he was the Lord's anointed. He would therefore rather flee for his own life than stretch out his hand to kill Saul. True, Saul disobeyed God's commandment and was rejected by God; this, however, was between Saul and God. David's responsibility before God was to be subject to the Lord's anointed.

David Maintained God's Authority

David stood absolutely for God's authority. It is just this trait which God desires to recover. Once, in the wilderness of Ziph, a similar occasion arose. The temptation to kill Saul came a second time: Saul lay sleeping and David found his way into his encampment. Abishai desired to kill Saul, but David forbade him and answered with an oath, "Who can put forth his hand against Jehovah's anointed, and be guiltless?" (1 Sam. 26.9) For the second time David spared Saul. He merely took away the spear and the jar of water which lay at Saul's head. This was a big improvement over the former instance, because this time he only touched things outside Saul's body, not something upon his body. David would rather be obedient to God and maintain God's authority than save his own life.

In 1 Samuel 31 and 2 Samuel 1, we read how Saul successfully attempted suicide with the help of a youthful Amalekite. The youth came running to David to seek a reward, saying that he had killed Saul. But David's attitude was still one of completely denying himself and submitting to God's authority. He spoke to the youth, declaring, "How wast thou not afraid to put forth thy hand to destroy Jehovah's anointed?" And he immediately ordered the young news bearer to be killed.

Because David maintained the authority of God, God acknowledged him as a man after His own heart. The kingdom of David continues until now; even the Lord Jesus is a descendant of David. Only those who are subject to authority can be authority. This matter is exceedingly serious. We must eradicate all roots of rebellion from within us. It is absolutely essential that we be subject to authority before we exercise authority. The church exists for the sake of obedience. She is not afraid of the weak ones, but she is afraid of the rebellious ones. We must subject ourselves to God's authority *in our heart* before the church can be blessed. Whether or not there is a future for the church depends on us. We are living in solemn days.

5 | The Obedience of The Son

Have this mind in you, which was also in Christ Jesus: who, existing in the form of God, counted not the being on an equality with God a thing to be grasped, but emptied himself, taking the form of a servant, being made in the likeness of men; and being found in fashion as a man, he humbled himself, becoming obedient even unto death, yea, the death of the cross. Wherefore also God highly exalted him, and gave unto him the name which is above every name; that in the name of Jesus every knee should bow, of things in heaven and things on earth and things under the earth, and that every tongue should confess that Jesus Christ is Lord, to the glory of God the Father. (Phil. 2.5-11)

Who in the days of his flesh, having offered up prayers and supplications with strong crying and tears unto him that was able to save him from death, and having been heard for his godly fear, though he was a Son, yet learned obedience by the things which he suffered; and having been made perfect, he became unto all them that obey him the author of eternal salvation. (Heb. 5.7-9)

The Lord Initiates Obedience

The Bible tells us that the Lord Jesus and the Father are one. In the beginning was the Word, and the Word was God. The heaven and the earth were made through the Word. The glory which God had in the beginning, even the unapproachable glory of God, was also the Son's glory. The Father and the Son exist equally and are equal in power and possession. Only in Person is there a difference between Father and Son. This is not an essential difference; it is merely an arrangement within the Godhead. Therefore the Scripture says that the Lord "counted not the being on an equality with God a thing to be grasped"—that is, a thing to be seized. His equality with God is neither something seized upon nor acquired, for inherently He is the image of God.

Philippians 2.5-7 forms one section and verses 8-11, another. In these two sections our Lord is seen as having humbled Himself twice: first He emptied Himself in His divinity, and then He humbled Himself in His humanity. By the time He came to this world, the Lord had so emptied Himself of the glory, power, status, and form of His divinity that no one then living, other than by revelation, knew Him nor acknowledged Him as God. They treated Him as a man, as an ordinary person of this world. As the Son He willingly submits to the Father's authority and declares that "the Father is greater than I" (John 14.28). Thus there is perfect harmony in the Godhead. Gladly the Father takes the place of the Head, and the Son responds with obedience. God becomes the emblem of authority, while Christ assumes the symbol of obedience.

For we men to be obedient it should be simple, because all we need is but a little humility. For Christ to be obedient, however, is not so simple a matter. It is much harder for Him to be obedient than for Him to create the heavens and the earth. Why? Because He has to empty Himself of all the glory and power of His divinity and take the form of a slave before He is even qualified to obey. Hence obedience is initiated by the Son of God.

The Son originally shared the same glory and authority with the Father. But when He came to the world He on the one hand forsook authority and on the other hand took up obedience. He willingly took the place of a slave, accepting the human limitation of time and space. He humbled Himself further and became obedient unto death. Obedience within the Godhead is the most wonderful sight in the whole universe. Since Christ was obedient unto death—suffering a most painful and shameful death on the cross—God has highly exalted Him. God exalts whoever humbles himself. This is a divine principle.

To Be Filled with Christ Is to Be Filled with Obedience

Since the Lord has initiated obedience, the Father has become the Head of Christ. Now because both authority and obedience have been instituted by God, it is natural for those who know God and Christ to obey. But those who know not God and Christ know neither authority nor obedience. Christ is the principle of obedience. He who accepts Christ accepts the principle of obedience. Hence a person who is filled with Christ must be one who is also filled with obedience.

Nowadays people often ask, "Why should I obey? Since both you and I are brothers, why must I obey you?" But men are not qualified to ask in this manner. The Lord alone is qualified; yet He has never said such words nor has such a thought ever entered His mind. Christ represents obedience, which is as perfect as the authority of God is perfect. May God be merciful to those who claim they know authority when obedience is yet missing in their lives.

The Way of the Lord

As regards the Godhead, the Son and the Father are co-equal; but His being the Lord is rewarded Him by God. The Lord Jesus Christ was made Lord only after He emptied Himself. His deity derives from who He is, for His being God is His inherent nature. His being Lord, though, issues out of what He has done. He was exalted and rewarded by God to be Lord only after He forsook His glory and maintained the perfect role of obedience. As regards Himself, He is God; as regards reward, He is Lord. His Lordship did not exist originally in the Godhead.

The passage in Philippians 2 is most difficult to explain, for it is most controversial besides being most holy. Let us remove our shoes and stand on holy ground as we review this Scripture. It seems as though at the beginning a council was held within the Godhead. God conceived a plan to create the universe. In that plan the Godhead agreed to have authority represented by the Father. But authority cannot be established in the universe without obedience, since it cannot exist alone. God must therefore find obedience in the universe. Two living beings were to be created: angels (spirits) and men (living souls). According to His foreknowledge God foresaw the rebellion of the angels and the fall of men; hence He was unable to establish His authority in angels or in the Adamic race. Consequently, within the Godhead perfect accord was reached that authority would be answered by obedience in the Son. From this come the distinctive operations of God the Father and God the Son. One day God the Son emptied Himself, and being born in the likeness of men He became the symbol of obedience. Inasmuch as rebellion came from the created beings, so obedience must now be established in a created being. Man sinned and rebelled; therefore the authority of God must be erected on man's obedience. This explains why the Lord came to the world and was made as one of the created men.

The birth of our Lord is actually God coming forth. Instead of remaining as God with authority He came to man's side, accepting all the limitations of man and taking the form of a slave. He braved the possible peril of not being able to return with glory. Should He have become disobedient on earth as a man, He would have still been able to reclaim His place in the Godhead by asserting His original authority; but if so, He would have forever broken down the principle of obedience.

There were two ways for the Lord to return: one way was to obey absolutely and unreservedly as man, establishing the authority of God in all things on all occasions without the slightest hint of rebellion; thus, step by step through obedience to God, He would be made Lord over all. The other way would be to force His way back by reclaiming and using the authority and power and glory of His deity because of having found obedience impossible through the weakness and limitation of human flesh.

Now the Lord discarded this second path and walked humbly in the way of obedience—even unto death. Once having emptied Himself, He refused to fill Himself again. He never took such an ambiguous course. Had the Lord failed in the way of obedience after having relinquished His divine glory and authority and taken the form of a slave, He would have never again returned with glory. Only by the way of obedience as man did He go back. Thus it was that He returned on the basis of perfect and singular obedience. Though suffering was added upon suffering, He displayed absolute obedience, without ever the slightest tinge of resistance or rebellion.

Consequently, God highly exalted Him and made Him Lord when He returned to glory. It was not *He* who filled Himself up with that which He had once emptied Himself of; rather, it was God the Father. It was the Father who was the One who brought this *Man* back into glory. And so God the Son is now also become Jesus the Man in His return to glory. For this reason, the name of Jesus is most precious; there is no one in the universe like Him. When on the cross He shouted "It is finished!", it proclaimed not only the accomplishment of salvation but also the fulfillment of all that His name signifies. Therefore, He has obtained a name which is above every name, and at His name every knee shall bow and every tongue shall confess that Jesus is Lord. Henceforward, He is Lord as well as God. His being Lord speaks of His relationship with God, how He has been rewarded by God. His being Christ reveals His relationship with the church.

To summarize, then: when the Son left the glory He did not intend to return on the basis of His divine attributes; on the contrary, He desired to be exalted as a man. In this manner, God has affirmed His principle of obedience. How necessary it is that we be wholly obedient without even the faintest trace of rebellion. The Son returned to heaven as a man; He was exalted by God after He was obedient in the likeness of men. Let us face this great mystery of the Bible. In bidding farewell to the glory and clothing Himself with human flesh, the Lord determined not to return by virtue of His divine attributes. And because He never gave the slightest appearance of disobedience, He was exalted by God on the ground of His humanity. The Lord set aside His glory when He came; but when He returned, He not only regained that glory but received even further glory.

Let us too have this mind which was in Christ Jesus. Let us all walk in the way of the Lord and attain to obedience by making this principle of obedience our own principle. Let us be subject to one another. Once having seen this principle, we will have no trouble discerning that no sin is more serious than rebellion and nothing is more important than obedience. Only in the principle of obedience can we serve God; only in obeying as Christ did can we reaffirm God's principle of authority, for rebellion is the outworking of the principle of Satan.

Learning Obedience through Suffering

It is told in Hebrews 5.8 that Christ "learned obedience through what He suffered." Suffering called forth obedience from the Lord. Please note here that He did not *bring* obedience to this earth; He *learned* it—and He did so through suffering.

When we meet suffering we then learn obedience. Such obedience is real. Our usefulness is not determined by whether or not we have suffered, but by how much obedience we have learned through that suffering. The obedient ones alone are useful to God. As long as our heart is not softened, suffering will not leave us. Our way lies in many sufferings; the easy-goers and pleasure-lovers are useless before God. Let us therefore learn to obey in suffering.

Salvation makes people obedient as well as joyous. If we seek only joy, our spiritual possessions will not be rich; but those who are obedient will experience the abundance of salvation. Let us not change the nature of salvation. Let us obey—for our Lord Jesus, having been made perfect through obedience, has become the source of our eternal salvation. God saves us that we may obey His will. If we have met God's authority we shall discover obedience to be easy and God's will to be simple, because the Lord Himself was always obedient and has given this life of obedience to us.

6 | How God Establishes His Kingdom

Though he was a Son, yet learned *obedience* by the things which he suffered; and having been made perfect, he became unto all them that obey him the author of eternal salvation. (Heb. 5.8-9)

And we are witnesses of these things; and so is the Holy Spirit, whom God hath given to them that *obey* him. (Acts 5.32)

But they have not all *obeyed* the glad tidings. For Esaias says, Lord, who has believed our report? (Rom. 10.16 Darby)

Rendering vengeance to them that know not God, and to them that *obey* not the gospel of our Lord Jesus. (2 Thess. 1.8)

Seeing ye have purified your souls in your *obedience* to the truth unto unfeigned love of the brethren, love one another from the heart fervently. (1 Peter 1.22)

The Lord Learned Obedience through Suffering

As God secured the principle of obedience through the life of our Lord, so God also established His authority through the Lord. Now let us see how God today establishes His kingdom on the basis of that authority. The Lord came to this world empty-handed; He did not bring obedience with Him. He learned obedience through what He suffered and thus became the source of eternal salvation to all who obey Him. By going through suffering after suffering He learned to be obedient unto death, even death on a cross. When the Lord came forth from the Godhead to become man, He truly became a man—weak and acquainted with suffering. Every suffering He bore ripened into a fruit of obedience. No suffering of any kind was able to stir Him to murmuring or fretfulness.

How different from this are the many Christians who fail to learn obedience even after many years. Although their suffering increases, their obedience does not. When suffering comes they often murmur with anguish, indicating again that they have not yet learned obedience. But as our Lord passed through all kinds of sufferings He continually exhibited the spirit of obedience; and so He has become the source of our eternal salvation. By the obedience of one man many have received grace. Our Lord's obedience is for the sake of God's kingdom. The aim of redemption is to further the kingdom of God.

God Will Establish His Kingdom

Have you noticed how greatly the fall of the angels and of man has affected the universe, what a great problem it has created for God? It was God's intention that the beings He created should accept His authority, yet both kinds of created beings rejected it. God could not establish His authority in the created beings; even so, He would not withdraw it. He might withdraw His presence, but He will never give up the authority He has initiated. Where His authority is, there is His rightful place. Hence God on the one hand will affirm His authority and on the other hand will establish His kingdom. Though Satan continually violates God's authority and men daily rebel against Him, God will not permit such rebellion to continue forever; He *will* set up His kingdom. Why does the Bible call God's kingdom the kingdom of the heavens? Because the rebellion has not been restricted simply to this earth, but has in addition reached to the heavens where the angels rebelled.

How, then, does the Lord establish God's kingdom? He establishes it through His obedience. Never once was He disobedient to God; never once did He resist God's authority while He was on earth. By obeying perfectly and by permitting God's authority to rule absolutely, He established God's kingdom within the realm of His own obedience. Now just as our Lord has done, so must the church today obey in order that the authority of God may prosper and the kingdom of God be manifested.

God Ordains the Church to Be the Vanguard of His Kingdom

After the fall of Adam God chose Noah and his family. However, they too fell—after the flood. So God called out Abraham to be the father of a multitude of nations, His intention being to set up His kingdom through Abraham. Abraham was succeeded by the election of Isaac and then later of Jacob. The descendants of Jacob multiplied greatly under the Egyptian oppression, and therefore God sent Moses to deliver them out of Egypt that they might establish a new nation. But because there were disobedient ones among them, God led the Israelites through the wilderness in order to teach them obedience. Nevertheless, they persisted in their rebellion against God, with the result that the whole generation fell dead on the way.

Even though the second generation succeeded in entering Canaan, they still did not hearken to God's word with a perfect heart; hence they could not drive the Canaanites completely out of the land. Saul became the first king, but due to his rebellion the kingdom could not be established. It was not until David was chosen that God found in him the king who was after His own heart, for David fully obeyed the authority of God. Even so, traces of rebellion still remained within the nation. God had appointed Jerusalem to be the place where His name would be set, but the people continued to sacrifice at the great high place in Gibeon. They were weak in obedience. They had a king yet they lacked the spiritual substance of a kingdom. Before the time of David there was a kingdom without a proper king. At David's time, both the king and the kingdom were present, but the spiritual substance of the latter was still missing. God's kingdom had yet to be truly established.

The Lord came to this world to set up God's kingdom. His gospel is twofold in nature: the personal and the corporate. As to the personal, the gospel calls men to receive eternal life through faith; as to the corporate, it bids men to enter God's kingdom through repentance.

God's eyes are on the kingdom: the so-called Lord's prayer, for example, begins and concludes with the kingdom. It starts with "Thy kingdom come, Thy will be done, as in heaven, so on earth." God's kingdom is that realm within which the will of God is carried out without any interference. The prayer ends with "thine is the kingdom, and the power, and the glory, for ever. Amen" (Matt. 6.13 margin). The kingdom and the power and the glory are interrelated. "Now is come the salvation, and the power, and the kingdom of our God, and the authority of his Christ," proclaims Revelation 12.10. This is because the kingdom is the scope of authority. "For lo, the kingdom of God is in the midst of you," says the Lord (Luke 17.21 margin). "In the midst of you", not "within you." The Lord Himself is actually the kingdom of God.

When the Lord Jesus is among you the kingdom of God is in your midst. This is because God's authority is completely carried out in His life. Now just as the kingdom of God is in the Lord, so is it to be found in the church—because the Lord's life is released to the church and so God's kingdom extends also to the church. Beginning with Noah God managed to get a kingdom, but it was earthy and not God's kingdom. God's kingdom actually begins with the Lord Jesus. How small was its scope at the outset. Today, though, this grain of wheat has borne much fruit. Its scope embraces not only the Lord but many saints as well.

God purposes that we be His kingdom and His church, since the church is ordained to be the sphere wherein God's authority is exercised. He wishes to have His rightful place in more than just a few individuals; He desires the whole church to give Him absolute preeminence in order that His authority may prevail and there be no rebellion. Thus will God set up His authority in the midst of His created beings. He wants us to be obedient not only to the direct authority which He Himself exercises but also to the delegated authorities whom He sets up. What He expects is full obedience, not a partial one.

Gospel Calls People Not Only to Believe but Also to Obey

The Bible mentions obedience as well as faith, for we are not only sinners but additionally sons of disobedience. What Romans 10.16 means by "believed our report" in Isaiah 53.1 is "obeyed the glad tidings" (Darby). The nature of believing the gospel is obeying it. "Rendering vengeance to them that know not God, and to them that obey not the gospel of our Lord Jesus" (2 Thess. 1.8). Those who do not obey are the rebellious: "Unto them that are factious, and obey not the truth . . .shall be wrath and indignation" (Rom. 2.8). The disobedient are the rebellious ones. "Seeing ye have purified your souls in your obedience to the truth" (1 Peter 1.22). This clearly indicates that purification is by obedience to the truth. Faith is obedience.

Believers would best be called "obeyers," for they are to be subject to the authority of the Lord as well as to believe in Him. After Paul had been enlightened he asked: "What shall I do, Lord?" (Acts 22.10) He not only believed, he in addition submitted to the Lord. His repentance was caused both by understanding grace and by obedience to authority. When he was moved by the Holy Spirit to see the authority of the gospel, he addressed Jesus as Lord.

God calls us not only to receive His life through faith but also to maintain His authority through obedience. He counsels us who are in the church to obey the authorities He has established—in home, school, society, and church—as well as to obey His direct authority. It is not necessary to point out specifically which person you should obey. It simply means that whenever you encounter God's authority, directly or indirectly, you should learn obedience.

Many are able to hearken to and obey only a certain person. This shows that they have not seen authority. It is vain to obey man; it is authority that we must obey. To those who know authority, even a slight disobedience will make them feel that they have been rebellious. But those who have not seen authority have no idea how rebellious they are. Before being enlightened, Paul kicked against the goads without realizing what he was doing. After enlightenment, however, the first thing which happens is that the eyes of Paul are opened to see authority, and this seeing continues to increase thereafter. Though Paul met only a little brother by the name of Ananias, he never questioned what kind of man Ananias was—whether learned or illiterate—because he was not looking at man. Paul recognized that Ananias was sent by God and he accordingly subjected himself to that delegated authority. How easy it is to obey after one has learned authority.

Through the Church the Nations to Become God's Kingdom

If the church refuses to accept God's authority God has no way to establish His kingdom. God's way of obtaining His kingdom is first in the Lord Jesus, then in the church, and lastly in the whole world. One day a proclamation will go out, announcing that "the kingdom of the world is become the kingdom of our Lord, and of his Christ" (Rev. 11.15). The church occupies the place between the kingdom found in the person of the Lord Jesus and the further extension of that kingdom to be found when the world becomes the kingdom of the Lord and of His Christ. The kingdom must be found in the Lord Jesus before it can be established in the church; it needs to be implanted in the church before it can be secured among the nations. There can be no church without the Lord Jesus, and there can be no further extension of God's kingdom without the church.

While on earth the Lord obeyed in even very minor matters. For example, He paid the temple tax. Having no money, He obtained the shekel from the mouth of a fish. Again, when asked on another occasion about paying civil taxes, He affirmed: "Render . . .to Caesar the things that are Caesar's, and to God the things that are God's" (Matt. 22.21). Although Caesar was a rebellious person, he was nonetheless set up by God; consequently, he must be obeyed. After we have fully obeyed, our Lord will then rise up and deal with those who disobey.

Through our obedience the kingdom shall be extended to the whole earth. Today, though, many are sensitive to sin yet not to rebellion. Men ought to have a sense for authority as well as a sense of sin. To be deficient in sensing sin deprives one from living as a Christian; to lack in sensing authority disqualifies him as an obeyer.

The Church Must Obey God's Authority

We must know how to obey in the church. There is no authority within the church which does not require obedience. God intends to have His authority fully manifested in the church and to have His kingdom extended through the church. After the church has fully obeyed, the entire earth shall be brought under the authority of God. Should the church fail to let God's authority prevail within it, God's kingdom will be thwarted from covering the whole earth. The church is therefore the way to the kingdom; but it can equally be the frustration to the kingdom.

How can God's kingdom be manifested if we are not able to be subject to a little hardship in the church? How can God's kingdom prevail if we always reason and argue among ourselves? We have greatly delayed God's time. All rebellion must be eradicated so that God's way may not be blocked. Once the church has truly obeyed, all nations will follow suit. The responsibility on the church is immense. When the will and command of God find free passage in the church, His kingdom shall surely come.

7 | Men Should Obey Delegated Authority

Authorities Instituted by God

1. IN THE WORLD.

> Let every soul be subject to the authorities that are above him. For there is no authority except from God. (Rom. 13.1 Darby)
>
> Be subject to every ordinance of man for the Lord's sake: whether to the king, as supreme; or unto governors, as sent by him for vengeance on evil-doers and for praise to them that do well. (1 Peter 2.13-14)

God is the source of all authorities in the universe. Now since all governing authorities are instituted by Him, then all authorities are delegated by Him and represent His authority. God Himself has established this system of authority in order to manifest Himself. Wherever people encounter authority they meet God. It is possible for men to come to know God through His presence; but even without His presence they can still know Him through His authority.

In the garden of Eden men knew God through His presence, or, during His absence, by remembering His command. Today though, men seldom encounter God directly in this world. (This, of course, does not apply to those in the church who live constantly in the spirit, for they often see God's face.) The place today where He manifests Himself the most is in His commandments. Only those who are foolish like the foolish tenants in the parable of Mark 12.1-9 have to have the personal presence of the Owner of the vineyard in order to obey, for in the story are not the servants and His Son sent ahead of Him as His representatives?

Those who are set up by God are to exercise authority for Him. Since all governing authorities are ordained and instituted by God, they are meant to be obeyed. If we would indeed learn how to obey God, we would then have no trouble recognizing on whom God's authority rests. But if we know only God's direct authority, we may possibly violate more than half of His authority. Upon how many lives can we identify the authority of God? Is there any room for us to choose between God's direct authority and His delegated authority? No, we must be subject to delegated authority as well as to God's direct authority, for "there is no authority except from God."

As to earthly authorities, Paul not only exhorts positively towards subjection but also warns negatively against resistance. He who resists the authorities resists God's own command; he who rejects God's delegated authorities rejects God's own authority. Authority, according to the Bible, is characterized by a unique nature: there is no authority except from God. He who resists authority resists God, and those who resist will incur judgment. There is no possibility of rebellion without judgment. The consequence of resisting authority is death. Man has no choice in the matter of authority.

During Adam's time God gave men dominion over the whole earth. What they were to govern, however, were the living creatures. After the flood God handed the power of governing man's fellowman to Noah, stating that "Whoso sheddeth man's blood, by man shall his blood be shed" (Gen. 9.6). From then on, the authority of governing man was invested in men. Ever since then there has been human government under which men are placed.

After having led His people out of Egypt into the wilderness, God gave them the Ten Commandments and many ordinances. Among these was one which declared: "Thou shalt not revile God, nor curse a ruler of thy people" (Ex. 22.28). This proves that God had put them under rulers. Even in Moses' time, the Israelites who resisted authority were actually resisting God.

Although the rulers of the nations did not believe in God and their countries were under the dominion of Satan, the principle of authority remained unchanged. Just as Israel was God's kingdom and King David was chosen by God, so the Persian Emperor was likewise said to have been set up by God. When our Lord was on earth He was subject to the governing authorities as well as to the authority of the high priest. He paid taxes and taught men to "render unto Caesar the things that are Caesar's" (Matt. 22.21). During questioning, when the high priest adjured Him by the living God to tell whether He was the Christ the Son of God, the Lord immediately obeyed (Matt. 26.63-64), thus acknowledging in all these instances that they were the authorities on earth. Our Lord was never a party to any rebellion.

Paul shows us in Romans 13 that all who are in authority are God's servants. We must be subject to the local authority under which we live, as well as to the authority of our own nation and race. We should not disobey local authority simply because we may be of a different nationality. The law is not a terror to good conduct but to bad. However different the laws of nations are, they are all derived from the law of God; the basic principle of all God's laws is to punish the evil and reward the good. All powers have their own laws. Their function is to maintain and execute their laws that the good may be approved and the bad disciplined. They do not bear the sword in vain. In spite of the fact that some powers do exalt evil and suppress good, they have to resort to distortion by calling the evil good and the good evil. They dare not come out openly and declare that the evil person is exalted because of his wickedness while the good one is chastened because of his goodness.

Up to the present, all powers are still following — at least in principle — the rule of rewarding the good and punishing the bad. This principle has not been changed; therefore the law of God remains in force. The day shall come when the lawless one who is the anti-Christ shall be in power; he then will distort the entire system of law and openly label the good as bad and vice versa. Then the good shall be killed and the evil shall be exalted.

The symbols for subjection to earthly authorities are four-fold: taxes to whom taxes are due, revenue to whom revenue is due, respect to whom respect is due, and honor to whom honor is due.

A Christian obeys the law not only to avoid God's wrath but also for the sake of conscience. His conscience reproves him if he is disobedient. Hence we must learn to be subject to local authorities. The children of God should not carelessly criticize or denounce the government. Even the police on the streets are instituted by God for they are commissioned to a specific task. When the tax-collectors or revenue inspectors come to us, what is our attitude towards them? Do we hear them as God's delegated authorities? Are we in subjection to them?

How difficult it is to obey if we do not see the authority of God. The more we try to obey the harder it becomes. "But chiefly them that walk after the flesh in the lust of defilement, and despise dominion. Daring, selfwilled, they tremble not to rail at dignities" (2 Peter 2.10). How many lose their power and forfeit their lives through reviling. Men should not fall into a state of anarchy. We need not be overly concerned with how God will deal with that which is done unrighteously, though we should pray for God's discipline on the ground of righteousness. In any event, insubordination to authority is mutiny towards God. If we are insubordinate, we will be a help to the principle of anti-Christ. Let us ask ourselves, When the mystery of lawlessness is at work are we a restraint or a help?

2. IN THE FAMILY.

> Wives, be in subjection unto your own husbands, as unto the Lord. For the husband is the head of the wife, as Christ also is the head of the church . . . But as the church is subject

to Christ, so let the wives also be to their husbands in every-thing. (Eph. 5.22-24)

Children, obey your parents in the Lord: for this is right. Honor thy father and mother (which is the first command-ment with promise), that it may be well with thee, and thou mayest live long on the earth. (Eph. 6.1-3)

Wives, be in subjection to your husbands, as is fitting in the Lord ... Children, obey your parents in all things, for this is well-pleasing in the Lord ... Servants, obey in all things them that are your masters according to the flesh; not with eye-service, as men-pleasers, but in singleness of heart, fearing the Lord. (Col. 3.18,20,22)

God sets up His authority in the home, but many of His children do not pay enough attention to this sphere of the family. Yet the epistles, such as Ephesians and Colossians which are considered the most spiritual letters, do not overlook this matter. They specifically mention subjection in the home, that without this there will be difficulty in the service of God. The letters of 1 Timothy and Titus deal with the subject of work, but they also speak of the family problem as being something which could affect the work. Peter's first letter focuses on the kingdom, but he too considers rebellion against familial authority as rebellion against the kingdom. Once the members of a family see authority many difficulties in the home will disappear.

God has set the husband as the delegated authority of Christ, with the wife as representative of the church. It would be difficult for the wife to be subject to her husband if she did not see the delegated authority vested in him by God. She needs to realize that the real issue is God's authority, not her husband. "That they may train the young women to love their husbands, to love their children, to be sober-minded, chaste, workers at home, kind, being in subjection to their own husbands, that the word of God be not blasphemed" (Titus 2.4-5). "In like manner, ye wives, be in subjection to your own husbands; that, even if any obey not the word, they may without the word be gained by the behavior of their wives" (1 Peter 3.1). "For after this manner aforetime the holy women also, who hoped in God, adorned themselves, being in subjection to their own husbands; as Sarah obeyed Abraham, calling him lord" (1 Peter 3.5-6).

"Children, obey your parents in the Lord" (Eph. 6.1), because God has set up the parents as authority. "Honor thy father and mother . . . that it may be well with thee, and thou mayest live long on the earth" (Eph. 6.2-3). Of the Ten Commandments this is the first one with a special promise. Some may die early because of their lack in paying filial honor, while others may be healed once their relationship with their parents is normalized. "Children, obey your parents in all things, for this is well-pleasing in the Lord" (Col. 3.20). To be subject to the parents requires a seeing of God's authority.

> Servants, be obedient unto them that according to the flesh are your masters, with fear and trembling, in singleness of your heart, as unto Christ; not in the way of eyeservice, as men-pleasers; but as servants of Christ, doing the will of God from the heart; with good will doing service, as unto the Lord, and not unto men. (Eph. 6.5-7)
>
> Let as many as are servants under the yoke count their own masters worthy of all honor, that the name of God and the doctrine be not blasphemed. (1 Tim. 6.1)
>
> Exhort servants to be in subjection to their own masters, and to be well-pleasing to them in all things; not gain-saying; not purloining, but showing all good fidelity; that they may adorn the doctrine of God our Saviour in all things. (Titus 2.9-10)

If we honor the authority of the Lord in our lives others will respect the Lord's authority in us. When Peter and Paul spoke these words slavery was at its worst in the Roman Empire. Whether slavery is wrong or right is not a problem for our consideration now, but we want to see that God has ordained that servants should obey their masters.

3. IN THE CHURCH.

> But we beseech you, brethren, to know them that labor among you, and are over you in the Lord, and admonish you; and to esteem them exceeding highly in love for their work's sake. Be at peace among yourselves. (1 Thess. 5.12-13)
>
> Let the elders that rule well be counted worthy of double honor, especially those who labor in the word and in teaching. (1 Tim. 5.17)
>
> Now I beseech you, brethren (ye know the house of Stephanas, that it is the firstfruits of Achaia, and that they have set themselves to minister unto the saints), that ye also be in subjection unto such, and to every one that helpeth in the work and laboreth. (1 Cor. 16.15-16)

God sets in the church authorities such as "the elders who rule well" and "those who labor in preaching and teaching." They are the ones whom everyone should obey. The younger ones in age must also learn to be subject to the older ones. The apostle exhorted the Corinthian believers to honor especially men like Stephanas whose family was the first converts in Achaia and who was willing to serve the saints with great humility.

In the church the women ought to be subject to the men. "I would have you know, that the head of every man is Christ; and the head of the woman is the man; and the head of Christ is God" (1 Cor. 11.3). God has arranged to have the men represent Christ as authority and the women represent the church in subjection. Therefore, the women ought to have a veil (Greek: authority) on their heads because of the angels (1 Cor. 11.10), and they should be subject to their own husbands.

"As in all the churches of the saints, let the women keep silence in the churches: for it is not permitted unto them to speak; but let them be in subjection, as also saith the law. And if they would learn anything, let them ask their own husbands at home" (1 Cor. 14.33-35). Some sisters ask, Supposing our husbands cannot answer our questions? Well, God tells you to ask, and so you ask. After awhile your husband will know, since being repeatedly asked he will be forced to seek for understanding. And so you help your husband as well as yourself. "Let a woman learn in quietness with all subjection. But I permit not a woman to teach, nor to have dominion over a man, but to be in quietness. For Adam was first formed, then Eve" (1 Tim. 2.11-13).

"All of you gird yourselves with humility, to serve one another" (1 Peter 5.5). It is most shameful for anyone to consciously display his position and authority.

God has also instituted authorities in the spiritual world. "But chiefly them that walk after the flesh in the lust of defilement, and despise dominion. Daring, selfwilled, they tremble not to rail at dignities: whereas angels, though greater in might and power, bring not a railing judgment against them before the Lord" (2 Peter 2.10-11). Here we are told of a most significant fact: that there are authorities and glorious ones in the spiritual world under whom angels are assigned. Although some of them have failed, the angels dare not revile them because once they were superiors. After their fall, though you may recount the fact of the fall, you may not add on your judgment, for fact plus judgment is reviling.

"But Michael the archangel, when contending with the devil he disputed about the body of Moses, durst not bring against him a railing judgment, but said, The Lord rebuke thee" (Jude 9). Why? Because at one time God had made Lucifer the chief of the archangels; and Michael, being one of the archangels, had been under his authority. Later Michael, in obedience to God, sought the body of Moses because one day Moses was to be raised from the dead (possibly at the Mount of Transfiguration). When

Michael was hindered by Satan, he could, in a rebellious spirit, have dealt with that rebellious one, Satan, by opening his mouth and reviling him. But he dared not do so. All he said was, "The Lord rebuke thee." (With men it is a different story, since God has never placed men under the authority of Satan. Though once we fell into his rule, we were never under his authority.)

On the same principle, David at one period submitted himself to the delegated authority of Saul. Subsequently, he still dared not overthrow Saul's fading authority. How dignified is delegated authority in the spiritual realm. It should not be despised; any reviling of it will result in the loss of spiritual power.

If you ever once in your life meet authority you will then be able to see God's authority everywhere. Wherever you go, your first question will be: Whom should I obey, To whom should I hearken? A Christian ought to have two senses: the sense of sin and the sense of authority. Even when two brothers consult together, though each may voice his opinion, only one makes the final decision.

In Acts 15 there was a council. The young as well as the old could rise up and speak. Every brother could offer his opinion. Yet after Peter and Paul had finished their words, James got up to give the decision. Peter and Paul only related facts, but James made the judgment. Even among the elders or the apostles there was an order. "For I am the least of the apostles," says Paul (1 Cor. 15.9). Some apostles are greater, some are lesser. This order is not arranged by man; nonetheless, each needs to know where he stands.

What a lovely testimony and beautiful picture this is. It is what Satan is afraid of, for eventually it will cause the downfall of his kingdom. For after we are all on the course of obedience God will come to judge the world.

Be Fearlessly Subject to Delegated Authority

What a risk God has taken in instituting authorities! What a loss God will incur if the delegated authorities He institutes misrepresent Him! Yet, undaunted, God has set up these authorities. It is much easier for us to fearlessly obey authorities than for God to institute them. Can we not then obey them without apprehension since God Himself has not been afraid to entrust authority to men? Even as God has boldly established authorities, so let us courageously obey them. If anything should be amiss, the fault does not lie with us but with the authorities, for the Lord declares: ' Let every soul be in subjection to the higher powers" (Rom. 13.1).

"Whosoever shall receive this little child in my name receiveth me" (Luke 9.48). For our Lord to represent the Father is no problem. The Father has confidence in Him and calls us to trust Him as we would trust the Father. But in the eyes of the Lord these children also represent Him. He has faith in these children and exhorts us to receive them as we receive Him.

When He sent out His disciples the Lord told them that "he that heareth you heareth me; and he that rejecteth you rejecteth me" (Luke 10.16). Whatever these disciples said or decided was reckoned as representing the Lord. How unafraid the Lord was in delegating His authority to them. He acknowledged every word which they spoke in His name. So that those who rejected them rejected Him. He did not forewarn the disciples not to speak carelessly. He was not at all apprehensive that they might do wrong. He had the faith and boldness to entrust His authority to them.

The Jews, though, were different. They doubted and questioned: "How can this be? How can we be sure that what you say is right? We need time to consider." They dared not believe and were much afraid.

Let us suppose you are the head of an institution. In sending a representative out, you tell him that you will acknowledge whatever he does according to his best judgment and that people listening to him will be considered as listening to you. Surely you will require him to report to you daily lest he make a mistake. But the Lord makes us representatives plenipotentiary. What confidence He has in us! Can we trust any less when our Lord displays such trust in His delegated authority?

People will perhaps argue, "What if the authority is wrong?" The answer is, If God dares to entrust His authority to men, then we can dare to obey. Whether the one in authority is right or wrong does not concern us, since he has to be responsible directly to God. The obedient needs only to obey; the Lord will not hold us responsible for any mistaken obedience, rather will He hold the delegated authority responsible for his erroneous act. Insubordination, however, is rebellion, and for this the one under authority must answer to God.

It is therefore clear that no human element is involved in this matter of authority. If our subjection is merely directed to a man the whole meaning of authority is lost. When God institutes His delegated authority He is bound by His honor to maintain that authority. We are each one of us responsible before God in this matter. Let us be careful that we make no mistake.

To Reject Delegated Authority Is an Affront to God

The entire parable recorded in Luke 20.9-16 focuses on the matter of delegated authority. God did not come personally to gather His due after He had rented the vineyard to the tenants. Three times He sent His servants and the fourth time He sent His own Son. These all were His delegates. He wanted to see if the tenants would be subject to His delegated authorities. He could have come and collected Himself, but He sent delegates instead.

In God's view, those who reject His servants reject Him. It is impossible for us to hearken to God's word and not to the words of His delegates. If we are subject to God's authority, then we must also be subject to His delegated authority. Other than in Acts 9.4-15 which illustrates the direct authority of the Lord, the rest of the Bible demonstrates the authority He has delegated to men. It may be said that He has given almost all His authority to men. Men may often think they are merely being subject to other

men, but those who know authority realize that these other men
are God's delegated authorities. It does not require humility to
be obedient to God's direct authority, but it does demand
humbleness and brokenness to be subject to delegated authority.
Unless one sets aside the flesh completely he is not able to receive and to hearken to delegated authority. May we realize that
instead of coming Himself, He sends His delegates to collect His
due. What, then, should be our attitude towards God? Should we
wait till God comes Himself? Remember that when He appears
He will come to judge, not to collect!

The Lord showed Paul how he had kicked against the goads
when he had resisted the Lord. Once Paul saw the light and saw
authority, however, he asked, "What shall I do, Lord?" By this
action he put himself under the direct authority of the Lord.
Nevertheless, the Lord immediately shifted Paul to His delegated
authority. "Rise, and enter into the city, and it shall be told thee
what thou must do" (Acts 9.6). From here on Paul recognized
authority. He did not consider himself so exceptional that he
would only listen if the Lord Himself told him what to do.
During their very first encounter the Lord put Paul under His
delegated authority. How about us? Since we have believed in the
Lord how much have we been subject to delegated authority? To
how many delegated authorities have we been submissive?

In the past God overlooked our transgressions because we
were ignorant, but now we ought to be serious about God's
delegated authorities. What God stresses is not His own direct
authority but the indirect authorities which He has established.
All who are insubordinate to God's indirect authorities are not in
subjection to God's direct authority.

For the convenience of explanation, we distinguish between
direct authority and delegated authority; to God, though, there is
but one authority. Let us not despise the authorities in home and
in church; let us not neglect all those delegated authorities.
Although Paul was stricken blind, he waited for Ananias with his
inner eyes wide open. To see Ananias was like seeing the Lord; to
hearken to him was like hearkening to the Lord.

Delegated authority is so serious that if one offends it he is at odds with God. No one can expect to obtain light directly from the Lord if he refuses to have light from delegated authority. Paul did not reason: "Since Cornelius asked for Peter, I will ask for either Peter or James; I will not have this little brother Ananias to be my authority." It is absolutely impossible for us to reject delegated authority and yet be subject directly to God; rejecting the first is the same as rejecting the second. Only a fool takes pleasure in the failure of delegated authority. He who dislikes God's delegate dislikes God Himself. It is the rebellious nature of man that makes him want to obey God's direct authority without being subject to the delegated authorities God has established.

God Respects His Delegated Authority

Numbers 30 deals with the matter of a woman's vow or pledge. While within her father's house in her youth a woman's vow or pledge was binding only if the father said nothing against it. If she were married, her vow had to be approved or disapproved by her husband. Direct authority would act upon what the delegated authority had consented to or it would annul what the latter had cancelled. God loves to delegate His authority and He also respects His delegate. Since the woman was under her husband's authority God would rather have her obey authority than maintain her vow. But if the husband as the delegated authority erred, God would surely deal with him, for he would bear her iniquity. The woman was not held responsible.

Thus this portion of the Scriptures tells us how we cannot bypass delegated authority to be subject to God's authority. Having delegated His authority to men, God Himself will not supersede delegated authority; rather is He restrained by the authority He has delegated. He confirms what delegated authority has confirmed and voids what it has also voided. God always maintains the authority which He has delegated. We are therefore left with no choice but to be subject to the governing authorities.

The whole New Testament stands behind delegated authority. The only exception is found in Acts 5.29 when Peter and the apostles answered the Jewish council which forbade them to teach in the name of the Lord Jesus. Peter answered by saying, "We must obey God rather then men." This was due to the fact that the delegated authority here had distinctly violated God's command and trespassed against the Person of the Lord. Such an answer as Peter's can only be given under this particular situation. In all other circumstances we must learn to be subject to delegated authorities. We can never bring in obedience through rebellion.

8 | The Authority of the Body

For as the body is one, and hath many members, and all the members of the body, being many, are one body; so also is Christ. For in one Spirit were we all baptized into one body, whether Jews or Greeks, whether bond or free; and were all made to drink of one Spirit. For the body is not one member, but many. If the foot shall say, Because I am not the hand, I am not of the body; it is not therefore not of the body. And if the ear shall say, Because I am not the eye, I am not of the body; it is not therefore not of the body. If the whole body were an eye, where were the hearing? If the whole were hearing, where were the smelling? But now hath God set the members each one of them in the body, even as it pleased him. And if they were all one member, where were the body? But now they are many members, but one body. And the eye cannot say to the hand, I have no need of thee: or again the head to the feet, I have no need of you. (1 Cor. 12.12-21)

And if thy brother sin against thee, go, show him his fault between thee and him alone: if he hear thee, thou hast gained thy brother. But if he hear thee not, take with thee one or two more, that at the mouth of two witnesses or three every word may be established. And if he refuse to hear them, tell it unto the church: and if he refuse to hear the church also, let him be unto thee as the Gentile and the publican. Verily I say unto you, What things soever ye shall bind on earth shall be bound in heaven; and what things

soever ye shall loose on earth shall be loosed in heaven.
(Matt. 18.15-18)

Authority Finds Its Fullest Expression in the Body

The fullest expression of God's authority is found in the
body of Christ, His church. Though God has established the procedure of authority in this world, none of those relationships
(rulers and people, parents and children, husbands and wives,
masters and servants) can give authority its fullest expression.
Because the many governing authorities on earth are all institu-
tional, there is always the possibility of the *appearance* of sub-
ordination without there being the real subjection of heart. There
is no way to detect whether the people are following an order of
the ruler from their hearts or merely rendering lip-service. It is
equally difficult to tell whether the children are hearkening to
their parents wholeheartedly or not. Hence subjection to authority cannot be typified by the way children are subject to their
parents, servants to their masters, or people to their rulers.
Though God's authority cannot be established without subjection, neither can it be if the subjection is not from the heart.
Then again, all these instances of subjection lie within the scope
of human relationships; consequently they are temporal and are
subject to separation. So it is clear that absolute and perfect
subjection cannot be found in them.

Only the relationship between Christ and the church can
fully express both authority and obedience. For God has not
called the church to be an institution; He has ordained her to be
the body of Christ. We often think of the church as a gathering
of believers with the same faith or as a meeting of loving hearts,
but God looks at her differently. She stands not only for the
same faith and united love but even more so as one body.

The church is the body of Christ, while Christ is the Head of
the church. The relationships of parents and children, masters
and servants, and even husbands and wives may all be severed,

but the physical head and its body are inseparable; they are forever one. In like manner, Christ and the church too can never be sundered apart. The authority and obedience found in Christ and the church are of such a perfect nature that they surpass all other expressions of authority and obedience.

In spite of the love parents have towards their children, they are liable to misuse their authority. Similarly, governments may issue wrong orders or masters may abuse their authority. In this world, authority as well as obedience are all imperfect. This explains why God desires to set up a perfect authority and a perfect obedience in Christ and the church, they being the Head and the body. Parents might even sometimes hurt their children, husbands their wives, masters their servants, and governments their people. But no head will do harm to its own body; the authority of the head is not subject to error, but is perfect. Likewise, the obedience of the body to the head is perfect. As soon as the head conceives an idea, the fingers move naturally, harmoniously, soundlessly. God's intention for us is that we render complete obedience; He will not be satisfied until we are brought to that same degree of obedience as is a body to its head.

This goes even beyond what can be represented by the relationship of husbands and wives, since husbands and wives are separate entities. But in Christ these two are one: He is the obedience as well as the authority. They are one in Him. This differs from the world, because in that sphere authority and obedience are two separate things. Not so the body and the head; movement of the body requires little effort from the head; the body moves graciously at the slightest impulse from the head. This is the kind of obedience which satisfies God, not the subjection children give to parents or wives to husbands, but such as the body renders to its head. How opposite this is from subjection through subjugation.

After one has learned more about obedience he will be shown the difference between God's command and God's will. The first is a word spoken by God while the latter is an idea conceived in God's mind. Command must be uttered but will can be silent.

The Lord Jesus moved in accordance with both God's will and His word.

In similar fashion God will work in His people until the relationship between Christ and the church fits the same pattern as the relationship between God and His Christ. God must continue laboring until we obey Christ as Christ obeys God. The first phase of God's work is to make Himself Christ's Head. The second phase is to make Christ the Head of the church. God will work till we obey His will instantaneously without even the need of being disciplined by the Holy Spirit. The third phase is to make the kingdom of this world the kingdom of our Lord and of His Christ. The first phase has already been accomplished, the third is yet to come. Today we are in the middle phase. Its fulfillment is absolutely essential for the coming in of the third phase. Are we here to obey so that God may have His way, or do we disobey and thus hinder God's work? God has been trying to establish His authority in the universe, and the key to it is the church. The church stands in the middle, serving as the pivot. In this, God clothes us with much more glory. Upon our shoulders rests the responsibility of manifesting authority.

For the Body to Obey the Head Is Most Natural and Agreeable

God has provided that the head and the body should share one life and one nature. It is therefore most natural for the body to obey the head. Indeed, in such a relationship disobedience would be strange. For example, it is normal for the hand to be raised at the instruction of the head; should the hand fail to respond, something would be wrong! In like manner, the spirit of life which God has given us is one and the same as that which the Lord has; so is the nature of our life the same as His. Thus there is no possibility of discord and disobedience.

In our physical bodies some movements are conscious while others are automatic, because the head and the body are so united that obedience includes both the conscious and the automatic. For instance, one can breathe a deep breath consciously or one can breathe naturally without any conscious effort. Our heart beats automatically; it does not wait for any order. This is the obedience of life. The head solicits the obedience of the body without noise or compulsion, void of conflict, and perfectly harmonious. But many people today will only obey commands. This is not adequate, for behind command lies the will, and in the will is the law of life. Now perfect obedience can only be reckoned as obeying the law of life. Anything less than what a body renders to its head cannot be taken as obedience. Forced obedience does not meet the yardstick of obedience.

The Lord has put us in His body wherein is complete union and perfect obedience. It is truly marvelous to see the mind of the Holy Spirit worked out in the members, who are not even conscious of being different members because their relatedness is so indivisible and their coordination so harmonious. Sometimes we do not even need to think in order to coordinate the functions of various members. It is truly beyond human words to describe the harmony which exists among the members. But let us each one be careful lest we be a sick, friction-causing member. By living under God's authority we should be able to obey most naturally.

In short, the church is a place not only for the fellowship of brothers and sisters but also for the manifestation of authority.

Resisting the Authority of the Members Is Resisting the Head

Though the authority of the body is sometimes directly manifested, it often is indirectly manifested. Not only is the body subject to the head; in addition, its various members help one another and are subject to one another. The left and the right hands do not have direct communication; it is the head which moves both of them. The left hand is in no position to direct the right hand, and vice versa. Neither can the hand order the eyes to look, but it merely notifies the head and lets the head give command to the eyes. Hence all the various members are equally close to the head. Whatever a member does is attributed to the head. When my eyes look, it is I who look; and so with my walking and working. We may therefore conclude that frequently the judgment of the member is the judgment of the head. The hand cannot see by itself; it must accept the judgment of the eye. For the hand to ask the head to look or for the hand to ask to see by itself is asking amiss.

Yet right here lies the common fault of God's children. We need to recognize in other members the authority of the Head. The function of each member is limited; the eye is to see, the hand is to work, and the foot is to walk; we must therefore learn to accept the functions of the other members. We ought not refuse the function of any member. If the foot should reject the hand, it is the same as rejecting the Head. But if we accept the authority of a member, it is the same as accepting the authority of the Head. By way of fellowship all other members can be my authority. Although the function of the hand of the physical body is tremendous, it has to accept the function of the feet when it comes to walking. The hand cannot feel color, so it needs to accept the authority of the eye. The function of each member constitutes its authority.

The Riches of Christ Is Authority

It is impossible to make each member a whole body; we must each learn to stand in the position of being a member and of accepting the workings of the other members. What others see and hear is reckoned as my seeing and hearing. To accept the workings of other members is to accept the riches of the Head. No member can afford to be independent, since each is but a member in the body; whatever the other members do is taken as the doing of all the members and hence the doing of the body.

Today's problem is that the hand insists on seeing, even after the eye has already seen. Everyone desires to have everything in himself, refusing to accept the supply of the other members. This creates poverty in him as well as in the church. Authority is but another expression of the riches of Christ. Only by accepting the functions of others—accepting their authority—does one receive the wealth of the whole body. Submitting to the authority of other members is to possess their riches. Insubordination brings in poverty. "If therefore thine eye be single, thy whole body shall be full of light" (Matt. 6.22); if your ear is good, the whole body will hear.

We often misunderstand authority as something which oppresses us, hurts us, and troubles us. God does not have such a concept. He uses authority to replenish our lack. His motive in instituting authority is to bestow His riches on us and to supply the need of the weak. He would not have you wait for decades and pass through many dark and painful days before you are able to see by yourself. By that time you might have led many into darkness. Indeed, you would become the blind leading the blind. What damage would God suffer through you! No, He first works in the life of another, and works thoroughly, so that He may give that person to you as an authority above you for you to learn obedience and to possess what you have never possessed before. This man's wealth becomes your wealth. Should you overlook this divine procedure, though you may live for fifty years, you may still lag far behind the attainment of that person.

The way God grants His grace to us is twofold: sometimes, though rarely, He grants grace to us directly; mostly He gives His riches to us indirectly—that is, God puts above you the brothers and sisters in the church who are more advanced spiritually so that you may accept their judgment as your judgment. This will then enable you to possess their wealth without you yourself having to go through their painful experiences. God has deposited much grace in the church; but He dispenses to each member some grace in particular, just as each star has its own particular glory. Hence authority brings in the riches of the church. The wealth of each member is the wealth of all. To rebel is to choose the way of poverty. To resist authority is to reject the means to grace and richness.

Distribution of Functions Is Also a Delegation of Authority

Who would dare to disobey the Lord's authority? But let us remember that the authority of the members which God has coordinated in the body needs to be hearkened to also. God has joined many members together, and it is downright rebellion for anyone to resist the help of the other members. Sometimes the Lord uses a member in a direct way, but at other times He uses another member to supply the need of that member. As the head directs the eye to look, the whole body must accept the seeing of that eye as its seeing. Such distribution of function is a delegation of authority; this also represents the authority of the head. Should the other members presume to see themselves, they are rebellious. Never be so foolish as to think of yourself as almighty.

Always remember that you are but a member; you need to accept the workings of the other members. When you submit yourself to a visible authority you are in perfect harmony with the Head, since the fact that someone has the supply constitutes his authority. Whoever is gifted has a ministry, and whoever has a ministry has authority. The eye alone can see; so in the need to see you have to submit to the authority of the eye and receive its supply. The ministry God appoints is authority; no one should reject it. Most people want to have God's direct authority, but God's more frequent way is to set up indirect or delegated authorities for us to obey. Through them we are to receive spiritual supply.

Life Makes Obedience Easy

It is hard for the world, even as it was for the Israelites, to obey, because there is no link of life. But for us who have a life relationship, to disobey is hard. There is an inward oneness—one life and one Spirit, the Holy Spirit directing and controlling everything. We are happy and restful if we are subject to one another. If we try to bear all the burden entirely upon our own shoulders, we will tire. But if the burden is distributed to various members, we will feel restful. How peaceful it is to accept the restraint of the Lord. In being subject to the authority of other members we experience a great emancipation. But to stand in another's place makes us feel most forced. To obey is natural; to disobey is difficult.

The Lord calls us to learn obedience in the body, the church, as well as in the home and in the world. Were we to learn well in the body, we would have no difficulty in other areas. The church is where we should begin to learn obedience. It is the place of fulfillment even as it is the place of trial. Should we fail here, we will fail everywhere. If we learn well in the church, the problems of the kingdom, of the world, and of the universe can be solved.

In the past both authority and obedience were objective, that is, an outward subjection to an outside power. Today authority has become a living thing, something inward. Authority and obedience meet each other in the body of Christ. Instantly both turn subjective and the two are merged into one. Herein is the highest expression of God's authority. Authority and obedience reach their consummation in the body. Let us be built up here; otherwise, there is no way. The place where we meet authority is in the body. The Head (the source of authority) and the members (each with its function, ministering to each other as delegated authority as well as being obedient to authority) are all in the church. If we fail to acknowledge authority here, there is no way.

9 | The Manifestations of Man's Rebellion

In what particular areas is man's rebellion most obviously manifest? In words, in reasons, and in thoughts. Unless there are practical dealings in these areas, the hope of deliverance from rebellion is very dim.

1. WORDS.

But chiefly them that walk after the flesh in the lust of defilement, and despise dominion. Daring, selfwilled, they tremble not to rail at dignities: whereas angels, though greater in might and power, bring not a railing judgment against them before the Lord. But these, as creatures without reason, born mere animals to be taken and destroyed, railing in matters whereof they are ignorant, shall in their destroying (margin, "corruption") surely be destroyed. (2 Peter 2.10-12)

Let no man deceive you with empty words: for because of these things cometh the wrath of God upon the sons of disobedience. (Eph. 5.6)

Yet in like manner these also in their dreamings defile the flesh, and set at nought dominion, and rail at dignities. But Michael the archangel, when contending with the devil he disputed about the body of Moses, durst not bring against him a railing judgment, but said, The Lord rebuke thee. But these rail at whatsoever things they know not: and what they understand naturally, like the creatures without reason, in these things are they destroyed (margin, "corrupted"). (Jude 8-10)

Ye offspring of vipers, how can ye, being evil, speak good

things? for out of the abundance of the heart the mouth
speaketh. (Matt. 12.34)

Words Are the Outlet of the Heart

A man who is rebellious in heart will soon utter rebellious
words, for out of the abundance of the heart the mouth speaks.
To know authority, one must first meet authority; otherwise he
will never obey. The mere hearing of the message of obedience is
totally ineffective. He must have an encounter with God; then
the foundation of God's authority will be laid in his life.
Afterwards, whenever he says a rebellious word—nay, even before
he utters it—he will become conscious of his trespass and thus be
inwardly restrained. If one can freely speak rebellious words
without any inward sense of restraint, he certainly has never met
authority. It is much easier to utter rebellious words than to
perform rebellious acts.

The tongue is hard to be tamed. Very quickly a man's
rebellion is expressed through his tongue. He may agree with a
person to his face but revile him behind his back; he may keep
quiet in front of a man but have much to say aloud later on. It is
not hard to use the mouth in rebellion. The people of today's
society are all rebellious; they only give lip-service and outward
subjection. The church ought to be different; in the church there
should be obedience from the heart. Whether or not there is
heart obedience can easily be detected by the words which come
from one's mouth. God looks for heart obedience.

Eve Carelessly Added to God's Word

When Eve was tempted, she added "neither shall ye touch it"
to God's word (Gen. 3.3). Let us realize how serious this is. One
who knows the authority of God would never dare add a syllable.
The word of God is clear enough: "Of every tree of the garden

thou mayest freely eat; but of the tree of the knowledge of good and evil, thou shalt not eat of it" (Gen. 2.16-17). God had never said "touch not"; this was added by Eve. All who easily change God's word, either by adding or by deleting, give evidence that they do not know authority; hence they are rebellious and untaught.

Suppose one is sent someplace by his government to be a representative and spokesman; surely that one will try hard to memorize what he has been commissioned to say; he would not dare add any of his own words. Although Eve saw God daily, she did not recognize authority; therefore she carelessly added her own words. Perhaps she figured there was not much difference in a few words more or less. No, even an earthly person serving an earthly master dare not freely change his master's words. How, then, dare we who serve the living God?

Ham Broadcast His Father's Failure

Let us see what Ham did when he saw his father's nakedness. He went out to tell it to his brothers, Shem and Japheth. He who is insubordinate in heart always expects the authority to fall. Thus Ham got his chance to reveal his father's fault. His doing so fully proved that he was not at all in subjection to his father's authority. Ordinarily he outwardly submitted to his father, but it was only half-hearted. Now, though, he had discovered his father's weakness, so he seized the opportunity to broadcast it to his brothers. Today many brethren, due to a lack of love, enjoy criticizing people and take great delight in disclosing others' faults. Ham had neither love nor subjection. He is a manifestation of rebellion.

Miriam and Aaron Reviled Moses

Numbers 12 records how Miriam and Aaron spoke against

Moses and dragged family affairs into the work. Moses occupied a unique position in God's calling; Miriam and Aaron were mere subordinates. This was God's ordering. Nevertheless, these two rebelled against that order and expressed their feeling by speaking against Moses. They did not know authority, since a knowledge of authority seals mouths and settles many problems. Natural difficulties are solved as soon as they encounter authority. Miriam merely said, "Hath Jehovah indeed spoken only with Moses? hath he not spoken also with us?" (verse 2). She did not seem to say much, yet God perceived that this was slanderous. Probably she had many more words still left unuttered, just as an iceberg has only one-tenth of its mass appearing on the surface while the other nine-tenths remain hidden in the water. However light the words may be, if there is a rebellious spirit within a person he will immediately be discovered by God. Rebellion usually manifests itself in words. No matter how light or how heavy these words are, it is rebellion.

Korah and His Company Attacked Moses

In Numbers 16 Korah and his company with two hundred fifty leaders of the congregation assembled themselves together against Moses. They attacked him with words. They uttered all which was in their hearts. They railed at Moses. Though Miriam spoke against him, her words were restrained; therefore she could be restored. But Korah and his company, like an uncontrollable flood, threw off all restraint. In this we see two different degrees of rebellion: some can be disgraced but finally restored, while some must be swallowed by Sheol, for they have no restraint whatsoever. These in Numbers 16 not only spoke against Moses but also openly censured him severely. The situation was so serious that Moses could do nothing but prostrate himself on the ground.

How grave was their accusation! They said to Moses, "Ye take too much upon you . . . Wherefore then lift ye up yourselves

above the assembly of Jehovah?" (verse 3) It was as if they were
saying, "We acknowledge that God is in the midst of the
congregation for the congregation is holy, but we do not
acknowledge your authority for you are a usurper." We learn
from this instance that *all who hearken to God's direct authority
but reject delegated authority are nonetheless under the principle
of rebellion.*

Were one submissive to authority he would surely control his
mouth; he would not dare speak so loosely. When Paul was
judged by the council he spoke as a prophet to the high priest,
saying, "God shall smite thee, thou whited wall" (Acts 23.3). But
he was also a Jew, so that as soon as he was told that Ananias was
the high priest he turned around and said, "I knew not, brethren,
that he was high priest: for it is written, Thou shalt not speak evil
of a ruler of thy people" (verse 5). How careful he was with his
words and how strictly he controlled his mouth.

Rebellion Is Linked with Fleshly Indulgence

The apostle Peter mentioned those who despise authority
immediately after he spoke of those who indulge in the lust of
defiling passion. The symptom of those who despise authority is
in speaking against, that is, in uttering rebellious words.

Like attracts like. A person will naturally mix with those like
him and communicate with those of a kindred nature. The
rebellious and the fleshly are joined together. God looks upon
them as equals. The rebellious and the fleshly are so bad and
willful that they are not afraid to revile the glorious ones. Those
who know God would tremble to do so. It is the lust of the
mouth to speak reviling words. Had one known God, he would
repent and abhor himself because he would know how much God
hates it. The angels were once under the jurisdiction of these
glorious ones, hence they dared not pronounce a reviling
judgment upon the latter before the Lord. They were cautious
not to harbor a rebellious attitude in dealing with those spirits

who had not remained in their former position.

For the same reason, we ought not revile others, speaking against them before God, not even in our prayers. David proved himself to be one who kept his position by acknowledging that Saul was the anointed of the Lord. Satan's power is established by those who do not keep their place, whereas the angels are those who do keep their place. Peter uses the angels to illustrate this principle of keeping in place so that we may be more careful about it.

There are two things which cause Christians to lose their power: (1) sin, (2) a reviling of authority. Each time one speaks out against another, it means loss of power. Loss of power is greater when disobedience is put into words than when it is hidden in the heart. The effect of words on power far exceeds our common notion.

It is true that in the sight of God a man's thought is judged as being equal to the act. He who conceives evil has already committed that evil. On the other hand the Lord says: "For out of the abundance of the heart the mouth speaketh . . . And I say unto you, that every idle word that men shall speak, they shall give account thereof in the day of judgment. For by thy words thou shalt be justified, and by thy words thou shalt be condemned" (Matt. 12.34,36-37). This implies that there is a difference between words and thought. Thought can still be covered, but once the word is spoken everything is bared. Christians today lose their power no less through mouth than through act; nay, they lose even more power through mouth. All rebellious ones have trouble with their mouths. Those who cannot control their words cannot control themselves.

God Strongly Rebukes the Rebellious

Read again 2 Peter 2.12. "But these, as creatures without reason, born mere animals to be taken and destroyed." Can there be any stronger words of rebuke in the Bible than those found here? Why chide them as animals? Because they are so insensitive. Authority being the most central thing in the whole Bible, reviling against it constitutes the gravest sin. Our mouth should not talk inadvertently. As soon as we meet God our mouth will be under restraint; we will not dare rail at authorities. Meeting authority creates in us an awareness of authority just as meeting the Lord makes us conscious of sin.

Difficulties in the Church Often Derive from Slanderous Words

Speaking inadvertently is largely responsible for the breaking of the unity of the church and the losing of power. Probably most difficulties in the church today are due primarily to slanderous words; only a minor part of the difficulties are real problems. In fact, most of the troubles in this world have been created through lies. If in the church we can stop slandering we will have eliminated the major part of our difficulties. How we need to confess our sins before God and ask for His forgiveness. All our words of reviling must be carefully and thoroughly terminated before God. "Doth the fountain send forth from the same opening sweet water and bitter?" (James 3.11) There ought not come from the same lips loving words and slanderous words. May God set a watch over our lips, and not only over our lips but also over our heart, that we be delivered from rebellious thoughts and reviling words. May reviling words forevermore depart from us.

2. REASONS.

> For the children being not yet born, neither having done anything good or bad, that the purpose of God according to election might stand, not of works, but of him that calleth, it was said unto her, The elder shall serve the younger. Even as it is written, Jacob I loved, but Esau I hated.

What shall we say then? Is there unrighteousness with God? God forbid. For he saith to Moses, I will have mercy on whom I have mercy, and I will have compassion on whom I have compassion. So then it is not of him that willeth, nor of him that runneth, but of God that hath mercy. For the scripture saith unto Pharaoh, For this very purpose did I raise thee up, that I might show in thee my power, and that my name might be published abroad in all the earth. So then he hath mercy on whom he will, and whom he will he hardeneth.

Thou wilt say then unto me, Why doth he still find fault? For who withstandeth his will? Nay but, O man, who art thou that repliest against God? Shall the thing formed say to him that formed it, Why didst thou make me thus? Or hath not the potter a right over the clay, from the same lump to make one part a vessel unto honor, and another unto dishonor? What if God, willing to show his wrath, and to make his power known, endured with much longsuffering vessels of wrath fitted unto destruction: and that he might make known the riches of his glory upon vessels of mercy, which he afore prepared unto glory, even us, whom he also called, not from the Jews only, but also from the Gentiles? (Rom. 9.11-24)

Slander Comes from Reason

Man's rebellion against authority is manifested in word, in reason, in thought. If he does not know authority he will speak slanderous words; such words usually issue out of his reason. Ham had his reason to slander his father, for Noah was naked. Miriam spoke against Moses on the basis of the fact of his brother's marriage to a Cushite woman. One who is subject to authority, however, lives under authority and not in reason. Korah and his company with two hundred fifty leaders reviled against Moses and Aaron saying, "All the congregation are holy, every one of them, and Jehovah is among them: wherefore then lift ye up yourselves above the assembly of Jehovah?" (Num. 16.3) They had their reason too; slanderous words like that usually are produced by reason.

Dathan and Abiram seemed to have an even stronger reason; they answered Moses by saying, "Moreover thou hast not brought us into a land flowing with milk and honey, nor given us inheritance of fields and vineyards: wilt thou put out the eyes of these men?" (verse 14) What they meant was that their eyes could see most clearly what the land was like there where they were. The more they pondered, the stronger their reason for distrusting Moses appeared to be. Reason cannot bear thinking, since it will only be aggravated further by the latter. People of this world live in reason. Wherein, then, are we any different from worldly people if we too live in that realm?

Following the Lord Demands Deliverance from Reason

It is very true that we need to have the eyes of our reason put out in order to follow the Lord. What governs our lives? Is it reason or is it authority? When one is enlightened by the Lord he will be blinded by the light, and his reason will be cast aside. Paul turned blind under the great light on the road to Damascus; no longer did he hold onto his own reason. Moses never had his eyes put out, nevertheless he acted as if he were blind. He had his arguments and his reasons, but in obedience to God he lived above reason. Those under the authority of God do not live by sight. The servants of God must be delivered from the life of reason. Reason is the first cause of rebellion; hence there can be no control over our words unless reason is thoroughly dealt with first. Unless one is delivered by the Lord from the bondage of reason, sooner or later he will utter slanderous words.

It sounds easy to talk about deliverance from the life of reason. But as rational beings how can we refrain from reasoning with God? It seems most difficult. We reason from childhood to adulthood, from our state as non-believers straight through until now. The basic principle of our life is reasoning. How then can we cease? To cease literally asks for the very life of our flesh! Hence there are two classes of Christians: those who live on the level of reason, and those who live on the level of authority.

Let us ask ourselves, Where do we live today? When God's command comes to us, do we stop and consider the matter to see if there are sufficient reasons for us to do it? Oh! This is nothing but a manifestation of the tree of the knowledge of good and evil. The fruit of that tree governs not only our personal affairs, even God's appointed things have to pass through our reason and judgment. We think for God and decide what God should think. Without doubt this is the principle of Satan, for is it not that he desires to be equal with God? All who really know God obey Him without argument; then there is no possibility of mixing up reason with obedience. If anyone wishes to learn obedience he must cast aside reason. He must either live by God's authority or live by human reason—it is absolutely impossible to live by both.

The earthly life of the Lord Jesus was entirely above reason. What reason could there be for the disgrace, the lashing, and the crucifixion which He suffered? But He submitted Himself to God's authority; He neither argued nor questioned; He only obeyed! To live under reason is so complicated! Consider the birds of the air and the lilies in the valley. How simply they live. The more we are subject to authority the simpler our lives will be.

God Never Argues

In Romans 9 Paul proved to the Jews that God also calls the Gentiles. He suggests that of the descendants of Abraham only Isaac was chosen and of the seed of Isaac only Jacob was chosen. All is according to the election of God. So why should not God choose the Gentiles? He can have mercy on whom He has mercy and compassion on whom He has compassion. He loves the treacherous Jacob and hates the honest Esau (at least this is what men surmise). He even hardens the heart of Pharaoh. Is He therefore unjust? But God sits on the throne of glory above and men are subject to His authority. Who are you, speck of dust, to argue with God?

He is God, and He has the authority to do what He likes. We cannot follow Him on the one hand and on the other hand demand to know the reason. If we desire to serve Him, we must not argue. All who meet God must throw away their reasonings. We can only stand on the ground of obedience. Let us not interfere through our arguments, trying to be God's counselors. Listen to what God asserts: "I will have mercy on whom I have mercy." How precious is the word "will". Let us worship Him. God never argues; He simply does what He wills. He is the God of glory. Paul also attests: "So then it is not of him that willeth, nor of him that runneth, but of God that hath mercy. For the scripture saith unto Pharaoh, For this very purpose did I raise thee up, that I might show in thee my power, and that my name might be published abroad in all the earth. So then he hath mercy on whom he will, and whom he will he hardeneth" (Rom. 9.16-18). To harden his heart does not mean to cause him to sin; it merely means to give him up (see Rom. 1.24,26,28).

Paul, foreseeing that they to whom he is writing may raise an objection, forestalls their argument by saying, "Thou wilt say then unto me, Why doth he still find fault? For who withstandeth his will?" (verse 19) Many would agree that the above reasoning is tremendously strong. Paul too knows the strength of such an argument. So he continues: "Nay but, O man, who art thou that repliest against God? Shall the thing formed say to him that formed it, Why didst thou make me thus?" (verse 20) He does not answer their argument; he asks them instead, "Who art thou?" He does not say, "What did you say?" He only asks, "Who art thou that repliest against God?" When God exercises authority He has no need to consult with you or gain your approval. He simply requires you to obey His authority and acknowledge that if this is of God, it is good.

Men always like to reason; but may we not ask, Is there any

real reason for our being saved? There is no reason whatsoever. I have neither willed nor run, yet I am saved. This is the most unreasonable thing which ever happens. But God will have mercy on whom He has mercy. The potter has the right over the clay to make out of the same lump one vessel for beauty and another for menial use. It is a matter of authority, not a question of reason.

The basic difficulty with us men today is that we are still living under the principle of the knowledge of good and evil, under the power of reasoning. Were the Bible a book of arguments then we certainly should reason everything. Yet in Romans 9 God opens the window of heaven and enlightens us not by arguing with us but by asking us, "Who art thou?"

God's Glory Delivers from Reason

It is not easy for men to be freed from slanderous words; it is harder still to be delivered from reasonings. When I was young I was frequently offended by the unreasonable things which God did. Later I read Romans 9, and for the first time in my life I touched a little of the authority of God. I began to see who I was—only a being created by Him. How dare I answer back to Him with my most reasonable words? He who is far above all lives in unapproachable glory. The glimpse of a fraction of His glory would send us to our knees and make us throw away our reasonings. Only those who live afar off can be haughty; those who sit in darkness can live by reasonings. But no one in all the world is able to truly see himself by the light of his own burning. Yet as soon as the Lord grants him a little light and permits him to see a little of God's glory, then he shall fall down as one dead—even as did the apostle John of old.

May God be merciful to us that we may realize once and for all how mean and low we are. Then we will not dare answer back to God. The Queen of the South was shown a little of the glory of Solomon and there was no more spirit left in her. A greater than Solomon is here; what matters my feeble reason?

Since the time when Adam sinned by taking the fruit of the tree of the knowledge of good and evil, reason has become the life principle of man. Only after the glory of the Lord appears to us do we realize that we are but dead dogs and lumps of clay. All our arguments will fade away in the light of His glory. The more a person lives in glory, the less he reasons. If anyone reasons a lot, we may know that he has never seen glory.

During these years I am beginning to learn that God often acts without reason. Even though I do not understand what He does I still learn to worship Him, for I am but a servant. Had I understood all His ways I myself would have sat on the throne. But once I see He is far above me—that He alone is the God on high—I prostrate in dust and ashes, all my reasonings disappearing. Henceforth authority alone is factual to me; reason and right or wrong no longer control my life. He who knows God knows himself and therefore is delivered from reason.

The way to know God is through obedience. All who still live in their reasonings have not known Him. The obedient alone truly know God. Herein is how the knowledge of good and evil which comes from Adam is eliminated. Thereafter it is relatively easy for us to obey.

"I Am the Lord Your God"—This Is the Reason

In Leviticus 18-22, each time God orders the people of Israel to do certain things, He interpolates a phrase: "I am the Lord your God." This is not even prefixed with the preposition "for." It means "I so speak because I am the Lord your God. I do not need to give any reason. I, the Lord, am the reason." If you see this you will never be able to live by reason any more. You will say to God: "Whereas in the past I lived by thought and reason, now I bow and worship You; whatever You have done, because it is You who have done it, is sufficient for me." After Paul fell on the road to Damascus his reasonings were all cast aside. The question he asked was, "What shall I do, Lord?" He instantly put himself in subjection to the Lord. No one who knows God will argue, for reason is judged and set aside by the light.

To argue with God implies that God needs to get our consent for all He does. This is utmost folly. When God acts He is under no obligation to tell us the reason, because His ways are higher than our ways. If we bring God down to reasonings we will lose Him because we make Him one of us. In reasonings we shall not have worship. As soon as obedience is absent, worship is lost. By judging God with our reason we set ourselves up as gods. Where, then, is the difference between the potter and the clay? Does the potter need to ask the consent of the clay in his work? May the glorious appearing of the Lord put an end to all our reasonings.

10 | The Manifestations of Man's Rebellion *(Continued)*

3. THOUGHTS.

> For the arms of our warfare are not fleshly, but powerful according to God to the overthrow of strongholds; overthrowing reasonings and every high thing that lifts itself up against the knowledge of God, and leading captive every thought into the obedience of the Christ; and having in readiness to avenge all disobedience when your obedience shall have been fulfilled. (2 Cor. 10.4-6 Darby)

The Link between Reason and Thought

Man manifests his rebellion not only in word and reason but in thought as well. Rebellious words come from rebellious reasoning, and reasoning in turn is "cooked up" in thought. Hence thought is the central factor in rebellion.

2 Corinthians 10.4-6 is one of the most important passages in the Bible, because in these verses the particular area in man where obedience to Christ is required is especially pointed out. Verse 5 says: "leading captive every thought into the obedience of the Christ." This suggests that man's rebellion is basically in his thought.

Paul mentions that we must destroy reasonings and every high thing that lifts itself up against the knowledge of God. Man likes to build reasons as strongholds around his thought, yet these reasons must be destroyed and thought taken captive. Reasons are to be cast aside, but thought is to be brought back. In spiritual warfare, the strongholds need to be stormed before the thought can be taken captive. If reasons are not cast aside there is no possibility of bringing man's thought into obedience to Christ.

The phrase "high thing" in verse 5 is "tall building" in the original. From God's viewpoint human reasoning is like a skyscraper, blocking out the knowledge of God. As soon as man commences to reason, his thought comes under seige and so is not free to obey God, since obedience is a matter of the thought. Reason expressed outwardly becomes words, but when the reasonings are hidden inside they surround thought and paralyze it from obedience. Man's habit of reasoning is so serious that it cannot be resolved without a battle.

Yet Paul did not use reason to fight against reason. The mental inclination to reason must be met with spiritual weapons, namely, the power of God. It is God who battles against us, for we have become His foe. Our mental habit of reasoning is something we inherited from the tree of the knowledge of good and evil, yet how few there are who realize how much difficulty these minds of ours give God. Satan employs all sorts of reasons to enslave us so that we, instead of being apprehended by God, become enemies of God.

Genesis 3 illustrates 2 Corinthians 10. Satan reasoned with Eve, and Eve, seeing that the tree was good for food, responded with reasoning. She did not listen to God, for she had her reasons. When reason arises, man's thought falls into a trap. Reason and thought are closely joined; the first tends to capture the second. And once the thought is taken captive, man finds himself incapable of obeying Christ. It therefore follows that if we really desire to obey God we must know how the authority of God destroys the strongholds of reason.

Recapturing the Captive Mind

In the Greek New Testament the word "noema" ("noemata", pl.) is used six times: Philippians 4.7; 2 Corinthians 2.11, 3.14,

4.4, 10.5 and 11.3. It is translated into English as "thought" or "thoughts"—meaning "the device(s) of the mind." "Mind" is the faculty; "device" is its action—the product of the human mind. Through the faculty of the mind man freely thinks and decides, and this represents the very man himself. Thus if one wants to preserve his freedom he has to say that all his thoughts are good and correct. He dare not open them to interference and hence must surround them with many reasonings. This is why men fail to believe in the Lord: they are so often imprisoned in the stronghold of some reasoning or other.

An unbeliever may say, "I will wait until I become very old"; or, "Many Christians do not behave too well. Therefore I cannot believe"; or, "Not yet. I will wait until my parents pass away." Similarly, there are reasons which believers may give for not loving the Lord: students will say that they are too busy with their lessons; businessmen are too occupied with their businesses; the un-well feel that their physical health is too poor, and so on. Unless God destroys these strongholds men will never be set free. Satan imprisons men by strongholds of reasonings. Most men are behind so many defensive lines that they are unable to break through to freedom. Only the authority of God can take every thought captive to obey Christ.

To know authority man's reasonings must first be overthrown. Not until man begins to see that God is God as stated in Romans 9 will his reasons be destroyed. And once Satan's strongholds are destroyed, no more reasoning will remain and man's thoughts can then be taken captive to obey Christ. Only after his thoughts are recaptured can man be truly obedient to Christ.

We may perceive whether or not one has met authority by observing whether his words, reasonings, and thoughts have been duly dealt with. Once one encounters God's authority his tongue dare not freely wiggle, his reasonings and, deeper still, his thoughts can no longer be loosely expressed. Ordinarily man has numerous thoughts, all fortified with many reasonings. But there must come a day when God's authority overthrows all the strongholds of reasoning which Satan has erected and recaptures all a man's thoughts so as to make him a willing slave of God. Where-upon he no longer thinks independently of Christ; he is wholly obedient to Him. This is full deliverance.

One who has not met authority often aspires to be God's counselor. Such a person does not have his thoughts recaptured by God. Wherever he goes, his first thought is how to improve the situation there. His thoughts have never been disciplined, hence his reasonings are so many and so unceasing. We must allow the Lord to do a cutting work in us, to cut to the very depth of our thoughts until they are all taken captive by God. Thereafter we will recognize God's authority and will not dare to freely reason or counsel.

We act as if there were two persons in the universe who are omniscient: God and myself. I am a counselor who knows every-thing! Such an attitude clearly indicates that my thoughts have yet to be recaptured, that I know nothing of authority. If I were one whose strongholds of reasonings had really been overthrown by God's authority, I could no longer offer counsel, nor would I have the interest to do so. My thoughts would be subordinate to God, and I would no longer be a free person. (Natural freedom is the ground of Satan's attack; it ought to be forfeited.) I would be willing to listen. Man's thoughts are controlled by either one of two powers: either by reasoning or by the authority of Christ. In fact, no one in this universe can freely exercise his will, because he is either captured by reasonings or apprehended by Christ. He consequently either serves Satan or serves God.

Whether or not a brother has met authority may be readily discerned by observing: (1) whether he has any rebellious words, (2) whether he reasons before God, and (3) whether he still offers many opinions. The overthrowing of reasonings is merely the negative aspect; its positive sequence is to have all one's thoughts taken captive to obey Christ so that he no longer offers his own independent opinion. Formerly I had many arguments to support my many thoughts; but now I have no more argument for I have been captured. A captive has no freedom; who would pay any attention to the opinion of a slave? A slave is to accept other's thoughts, not to offer his own opinion. Consequently we who are captured by Christ are ready to accept God's thoughts and not to offer any counsel of our own.

Warnings to the Opinionated

1. PAUL.

In the natural, Paul was a clever, capable, wise, and rational person. He could always find a way to do things, he had confidence, and he served God with all his enthusiasm. But while he was heading a group of people on their way to Damascus to seize the Christians there, he was smitten to the ground by a great light. Then and there all his intentions, ways, and ability were dissolved. He neither returned to Tarsus nor went back to Jerusalem. He had not only abandoned his task in Damascus but he had also cast away all his reasons for it.

Many when they encounter difficulty change their direction, trying first this way and then that; but no matter what they do they are still going on according to their own ways and ideas. They are so foolish as not to fall after they have been smitten by God. Though God has prostrated them in that particular thing, they will not be smitten as to their reasonings and thoughts. Thus, many may indeed have their road to Damascus blocked, yet they still retain their ways to Tarsus or to Jerusalem.

Not so with Paul. Once he was smitten, he lost everything. He could neither say nor think of anything. He knew nothing at all. "What shall I do, Lord?" he asked. Here we find one whose thoughts had been taken captive by the Lord and who obeyed from the depth of his heart. Formerly, no matter what the circumstance, Saul of Tarsus always took the lead; but now, having met the authority of God, Paul lost his opinions. The primary evidence that one has met God is in the disappearing of one's opinions and cleverness. May we honestly ask God to grant us the bewilderment of light. Paul seemed to say: "I am a man recaptured by God and thus a prisoner of the Lord. It is now the time for me to listen and obey, not to think and decide."

2. KING SAUL.

King Saul was rejected by God not because of stealing but because of sparing the best of the sheep and of the oxen to sacrifice to the Lord. This was something which came from his own opinion—his own thoughts of how to please God. His rejection was due to his thoughts being uncaptured by God. No one could say that King Saul was not zealous in serving God. He did not lie, since he actually *had* spared the best of the cattle and sheep. But he had made his decision according to his own thought. (See 1 Sam. 15)

The inference is clear: all who serve God must categorically refrain from making decisions on the basis of their own thoughts; rather, they are to execute the will of God. They should expectantly say, "Lord, what do You want me to do?" To say more would be totally wrong. To obey is better than to sacrifice. Men have absolutely no right to offer counsel to God.

When King Saul saw these sheep and cattle, he wished to spare them for sacrifice. His heart may have been towards God, yet he was lacking in the spirit of obedience. A heart towards God cannot replace the attitude of "I dare not say anything"; an offering of fat cannot supersede "making no voice." Because King Saul refused to destroy all of the Amalekites with their sheep and cattle as God had commanded, he was to be slain by an Amalekite and his rule thereby terminated. All who spare the Amalekite out of their own thought will finally be killed by an Amalekite.

3. NADAB AND ABIHU.

Nadab and Abihu became rebels in the matter of the offering

because they failed to be subject to their father's authority. They tried to carry out their own thoughts. They sinned against God by offering strange fire; thus they offended the administration of God. Though they neither spoke one word nor offered any reasons, nevertheless they burned incense according to their own thought and feeling. They considered such service as doing a good thing; that if they erred it would only be erring on the side of doing a good thing—namely, serving God. They thought such sin was insignificant. But they did not know they would be outrightly rejected by God and punished with death.

Testimony of the Kingdom Brought In through Obedience

God does not look at how fervently we preach the gospel or how willingly we suffer for Him; He looks to see how obedient we are. God's kingdom begins when there is an absolute obedience to God—no voicing of opinion, no presenting of reasonings, no murmuring, no reviling. For this glorious day God has waited since the creation of the world. Although God has His first-born Son who is the first-fruit of obedience, He is waiting for His many sons to be like the First-born. Wherever there is a church on this earth which truly obeys God's authority, there is the testimony of the kingdom and there Satan is defeated. Satan is not afraid of our work so long as we act on the principle of rebellion. He only laughs in secret when we do things according to our own thoughts.

The Mosaic law stated that the ark must be borne by the Levites, but the Philistines sent the ark back to Israel by putting it on an ox-cart. David, in transporting the ark to his city, failed to consult God. Instead, he ordered according to his own thought that it should be brought up by ox-cart. The oxen stumbled and the ark began to fall. Uzzah put out his hand toward the ark of God and took hold of it. Instantly he was stricken to death by God. Even if the ark had not fallen, it was not upon the shoulders of the Levites where it belonged, but upon an ox-cart.

At an earlier time when the ark was borne by the Levites through the River Jordan it was safe and secure in spite of the overflow of the river. The contrast shows us that God wants us to obey Him, not to suggest our thoughts to Him. God must empty us before His will can be carried out without interference. The way of service is forever blocked if we bring in man's thoughts. God must rule; men must not give counsel.

Hence man's thoughts must be totally cast aside. In the past we found freedom in living by ourselves; now we find true freedom in having our thoughts recaptured by God to the obedience of Christ. In losing our freedom, we gain true freedom in the Lord.

"Being in readiness to avenge all disobedience, when your obedience shall be made full" (2 Cor. 10.6). Perfect obedience is possible only after the thoughts are recaptured. All who still incline to offer counsel to God are not fully obedient. The Lord is ready to avenge all disobedience when our obedience has been completed. If we as a company of believers can turn so thoroughly as to obey God absolutely, fearing our own ideas and opinions, then God will be able to manifest His authority on earth. How can we expect the world to be obedient if the church does not obey? A disobedient church cannot expect unbelievers to obey the gospel. But with an obedient church there will also come obedience to the gospel.

We must all learn to accept discipline that our mouths may be so instructed as not to speak loosely, our mind not to argue, and our hearts not to offer counsel. The way of glory is just ahead of us. God shall manifest his authority on this earth.

11 | The Measure of Obeying Authority

By faith Moses, when he was born, was hid three months by his parents, because they saw he was a goodly child; and they were not afraid of the king's commandment. (Heb. 11.23)

But the midwives feared God, and did not as the king of Egypt commanded them, but saved the men-children alive. (Ex. 1.17)

If it be so, our God whom we serve is able to deliver us from the burning fiery furnace; and he will deliver us out of thy hand, O king. But if not, be it known unto thee, O king, that we will not serve thy gods, nor worship the golden image which thou hast set up. (Dan. 3.17-18)

And when Daniel knew that the writing was signed, he went into his house; (now his windows were open in his chamber toward Jerusalem;) and he kneeled upon his knees three times a day, and prayed, and gave thanks before his God, as he did aforetime. (Dan. 6.10)

Now when they were departed, behold, an angel of the Lord appeareth to Joseph in a dream, saying, Arise and take the young child and his mother, and flee into Egypt, and be thou there until I tell thee: for Herod will seek the young child to destroy him. (Matt. 2.13)

But Peter and the apostles answered and said, We must obey God rather than men. (Acts 5.29)

Submission Is Absolute, but Obedience Is Relative

Submission is a matter of attitude, while obedience is a matter of conduct. Peter and John answered the Jewish religious council: "Whether it is right in the sight of God to hearken unto you rather than unto God, judge ye" (Acts 4.19). Their spirit was not rebellious, since they still submitted to those who were in authority. Obedience, however, cannot be absolute. Some authorities must be obeyed; while others should not be, especially in matters which touch upon Christian fundamentals—such as believing the Lord, preaching the gospel, and so forth. Children may make suggestions to their parents, yet they must not show an unsubmissive attitude. Submission ought to be absolute. Sometimes obedience is submission, whereas at other times an inability to obey may still be submission. Even when making a suggestion, we should maintain an attitude of submission.

Acts 15 serves as a good example of how the church meets. During the meeting there may be suggestions and debates, but once the decision is made all must learn to submit.

The Measure of Obeying Delegated Authorities

If parents should refuse to let their children gather with the saints, the children must maintain an attitude of submission though they may not necessarily obey. This is similar to the way the apostles responded to the Jewish council. When they were forbidden by the council to preach the gospel they kept a submissive spirit throughout the trial; even so, they continued on with the Lord's commission. They did not disobey with quarrels and shoutings, they only quietly and softly dissented. There absolutely should neither be a word of slander nor an attitude of insubordination towards the governing authorities. One who knows authority will be soft and tender. He will be absolute in his submission both in his heart, in his attitude, and in his word. There will be no signs of harshness or rebellion.

When delegated authority (men who represent God's authority) and direct authority (God Himself) are in conflict, one can render submission but not obedience to the delegated authority. Let us summarize this under three points:

1. Obedience is related to conduct; it is relative. Submission is related to heart attitude: it is absolute.

2. God alone receives unqualified obedience without measure; any person lower than God can only receive qualified obedience.

3. Should the delegated authority issue an order clearly contradicting God's command, he will be given submission but not obedience. We should submit to the *person* who has received delegated authority from God, but we should disobey the order which offends God.

If parents want you as their children to go to some place where you as a Christian would rather not go (but not to a place where the question of sin would be involved), then the matter is open for discussion. Submission is absolute, while obedience may be a matter for consideration. Should the parents compel you to go, you go. But if they do not insist, then you are free not to go. God will deliver you from your environment if you as children maintain a right attitude.

Examples in the Bible

1. The midwives and Moses' mother both disobeyed the decree of Pharaoh by preserving Moses alive. Yet they were considered to be women of faith.

2. The three friends of Daniel refused to bow to the golden image set up by King Nebuchadnezzar. They disobeyed the king's order, yet they submitted to the king's fire.

3. In disregard of the royal decree Daniel prayed to God; nevertheless he submitted to the king's judgment by being thrown into the lions' den.

4. Joseph took the Lord Jesus and fled to Egypt to avoid having the child killed by King Herod.

5. Peter preached the gospel though it was against the command of the ruling council, for he said it was right to obey God rather than men. Yet he allowed himself to be taken into prison.

Indispensable Signs Accompanying the Obedient

How can we judge whether a person is obedient to authority? By the following signs:

1. A person who has known authority will naturally try to find authority wherever he goes. The church is the place where obedience can be learned, since there is not really such a thing as obedience in this world. Only Christians can obey, and they too must learn to obey—not outwardly, but from the heart. Yet once this lesson of obedience has been learned, the Christian will look for and find authority everywhere.

2. A person who has met God's authority is soft and tender. He has been melted and is not able to be hard. He is afraid of being wrong and thus he is soft.

3. A person who has truly met authority never likes to be in authority. He has neither the thought nor the interest to become one in authority. He does not take delight in giving counsel, nor does he take pleasure in controlling others. The truly obedient is always in fear of making an error. But alas, how many there are who still aspire to be God's counselors. Only those who do not know authority are those who wish to be authorities.

4. A person who has contacted authority keeps his mouth closed. He is under restraint. He dare not speak carelessly because there is in him a sense of authority.

5. A person who has touched authority is sensitive to each act of lawlessness and rebellion around him. He sees how the principle of lawlessness has filled the earth and even the church. Only those who have experienced authority can lead others into obedience. Brothers and sisters must learn to obey authority; otherwise the church will not have any testimony on earth.

Maintenance of Order Is in the Knowing of Authority

Unless men are brought into living touch with authority, it is impossible to establish the obedience and the authority which

issue from the principle of obedience to authority. For instance,
if you put two dogs together it is useless to try to establish one
of them as the authority and the other as the one who obeys.
Only a living contact with authority can solve the problems
issuing from a lack of obedience to authority. And as soon as one
offends authority, he will be instantly conscious of having offended God. It is futile to point out error to one who has never
seen authority. No, first lead him to know authority and then
you can show him his fault. In helping others, though, you must
beware lest you too fall into their rebellion.

Now was it right for Martin Luther to stand up and speak for
the fundamental principle of justification by faith? Yes, for he
was obeying God in standing for the truth. Likewise is it proper
for us too to stand for the truth, such as the testimony of the
oneness of the local church, leaving behind denominational
ground. We have seen the body of Christ and the glory of Christ;
and thus we cannot take upon ourselves any name other than
Christ's. The name of the Lord is important. Why do we not say
"saved by the blood" but rather "saved by the name of the
Lord"? Because the name of the Lord speaks also of His resurrection and ascension. "For neither is there any other name under
heaven, that is given among men, wherein we must be saved"
(Acts 4.12). We are baptized in the name of the Lord, and we
gather unto His name too. Therefore the cross and the blood
alone cannot solve the problem of denominations. But when we
have once seen the glory of the ascended Lord we can no longer
insist on having any other name but the Lord's. Then we can
only lift up the Lord's name, refusing to have any other. The
organized denominations of today are an affront to the glory of
the Lord.

Life and Authority

The church is maintained by two essentials: life and authority. The indwelling life we have received is a life of submission,

enabling us to obey authority. Difficulties within the church are rarely found in matters of outward disobedience; mostly they are related to a lack of inward submission. But the governing principle of our life ought to be submission, just as that of birds is to fly and that of fish is to swim.

"The unity of the faith, and of the knowledge of the Son of God" found in Ephesians 4.13 seems to be still so far away; yet it is not actually that far off if we have known authority. Saints may possess different opinions and yet there still be no insubordination, for even with differing opinions we can nonetheless submit to one another. Thus are we one in the faith. Today we already have the indwelling life and we have touched something of the governing principle of that life; hence, if God be merciful to us, let us speedily move on. The life we have received is not only for dealing with sin—the negative side—but more is it for obeying—the vital and positive side. When the spirit of rebellion leaves us, then will the spirit of obedience be quickly restored to the church, and the sublime state of Ephesians 4 shall then be ushered in. If all the local churches walk in this way of obedience, the glorious fact of the unity of the faith will verily appear before our eyes.

PART TWO

DELEGATED AUTHORITIES

Obeying Delegated Authorities and Being a Delegated Authority

God's children should not only learn to recognize authority, they should likewise be looking for those to whom they ought to be obedient. The centurion spoke to the Lord Jesus, saying: "I also am a man under authority, having under myself soldiers" (Matt. 8.9). He was truly a man who knew authority. Today, even as God upholds the whole universe with His authority, so He joins His children together through His authority. If any one of His children is independent and self-reliant, not subject to God's delegated authority, then that one can never accomplish the work of God on earth. Each and every child of God must look for some authority to obey so that he or she may be well coordinated with others. Sad to say, though, many have failed at this point.

How can we believe if we do not know whom to believe; how can we love if we do not know whom to love; or how then can we obey if we do not know whom to obey? Yet in the church there are many delegated authorities to whom we owe our submission. By submitting to them we submit to God. We are not to choose whom to obey, but to learn to be subject to all governing authorities.

There is no one who is fit to be God's delegated authority unless he himself first knows how to be under authority. No one can know how to exercise authority until his own rebellion has been dealt with. God's children are not a heap of yarn or a mixed multitude. If there is no testimony of authority, there is no church nor work. This poses a serious problem. It is essential that we learn to be subject to one another and subject to delegated authorities.

Three Requirements for a Delegated Authority

Beyond a personal knowledge of authority and a life lived under authority, God's delegated authority needs to fulfill the three following principal requirements:

1. He must know that all authority comes from God. Every person who is called to be a delegated authority should remember that "there is no authority except from God; and those that exist are set up by God" (Rom. 13.1 Darby). He himself is not the authority, nor can anyone make of himself an authority. His opinions, ideas and thoughts are no better than those of others. They are utterly worthless. Only what comes from God constitutes authority and commands man's obedience. A delegated authority is to represent God's authority, never to assume that he too has authority.

We ourselves have not the slightest authority in the home, the world, or the church. All we can do is execute God's authority; we cannot create authority for ourselves. The policeman and the judge execute authority and enforce the law, but they should not write the law themselves. Likewise, those who are placed in authority in the church merely represent God's authority · Their authority is due to their being in a representative capacity, not because they in themselves have any merit more excellent than the rest.

For one to be in authority does not depend on his having ideas and thoughts; rather does it hinge on knowing the will of God. The measure of one's knowledge of God's will is the measure of his delegated authority. God establishes a person to be His delegated authority entirely on the basis of that person's knowledge of God's will. It has nothing at all to do with having many ideas, strong opinions, or noble thoughts. Indeed, such persons who are strong in themselves are greatly to be feared in the church.

Many young brothers and sisters are as yet unlearned, not knowing God's will; hence God has put them under authority. Those in authority are responsible to instruct these younger ones in the knowledge of God's will. However, in each and every dealing with them, it is imperative for the delegated authority to know beyond doubt what the Lord's will is in that particular affair. Then he may act as God's representative and minister with authority. Apart from such knowledge, he has no authority to command obedience.

No one is able to be God's delegated authority unless he has learned to obey God's authority and understand His will. To illustrate. If a man represents a certain company in negotiating a business contract, before he signs the contract he must first consult with his general manager; he cannot sign the agreement independently. Similarly, one who acts as God's delegated authority needs to first know the will and the way of God before he is able to put authority into effect. He can never give to the brothers and sisters an order which God has not given. Were he to tell others what to do and yet not have it acknowledged by God, he would be representing himself and not God. Hence it is required of him that he first know God's will before he acts on God's behalf. Then shall his action come under God's approval. Only God's acknowledged judgment is authoritative; whatever comes from man is wholly void of authority, for it can only represent himself.

For this reason we must learn to rise high and touch deeply in spiritual things. We need to have a more abundant knowledge of God's will and way. We should see what others have not seen and attain to what others have not attained. What we do must come from what we have learned before God, and what we say must issue from that which we have experienced of Him. There is no authority except God. If we have seen nothing before God, then we have absolutely no authority before men. All authority depends on what we have learned and known before God. Do not think that because one is older he can suppress the younger, because one is a brother he can oppress the sisters, or because one is quick-tempered he can subdue the slow in temper. To try to do this will not be successful. Whoever wishes that others be subject to authority must himself first learn to know God's authority.

2. He must deny himself. Until one knows the will of God he should keep his mouth shut. He should not exercise authority carelessly. He who is to represent God must learn on the positive side what God's authority is and on the negative side how to deny himself. Neither God nor the brothers and sisters will treasure your thoughts. Probably you yourself are the only one in the whole world who considers your opinion as the best. Persons with many opinions, ideas, and subjective thoughts are to be feared. They like to be counselors to all. They seize upon every opportunity to press their ideas on others. God can never use a person so full of opinions, ideas, and thoughts as the one to represent His authority. For example, who would ever employ a spendthrift to keep his accounts? To do so would be to invite acute suffering. Nor will God engage a man of many opinions to be His delegated authority lest He too should suffer damage.

Unless we are completely broken by the Lord we are not qualified to be God's delegated authority. God calls us to *represent* His authority, not to *substitute* His authority. God is sovereign in His personality and position. His will is His. He never consults with man nor does He allow anyone to be His counselor. Consequently, one who represents authority must not be a subjective person.

This is not to imply that before he can be used by God he must be reduced to having no opinion, no thought, and no judgment. Not at all. It merely means that the man must be truly broken; his cleverness and his opinions and his thoughts must all be broken. Those who are naturally talkative, opinionated, and self-conceited need a radical dealing, a basic bending. This is something which cannot be either a doctrine or an imitation. It must be wounds in the flesh. Only after one is scourged by God does he begin to live in fear and trembling before Him. He dare not open his mouth inadvertently. Were his experience nothing more than doctrine or imitation, then as time goes on the fig leaves will soon dry up (Gen. 3.7) and his original state will reappear. It is futile for us to control ourselves by our own will. In our much talking we will soon forget ourselves and expose the

ical self. How we need to be slain by God's light. Like Balaam in Numbers 22.25, we need to be pushed against the wall and to have our foot crushed. We will then feel pained as we move and will dare not speak casually. It is not necessary to advise one, whose foot is crushed, to walk slowly. Only by such painful experiences as this shall we be delivered from ourselves.

As a delegated authority we are not to express our own views nor to itch to interfere with others' affairs. Some seem to consider themselves as supreme court justices. They pretend to know everything in the church and everything in the world. They have a ready opinion on anybody and everything, freely dispensing their teachings as if they were the gospel. A subjective person has never learned discipline, nor has he ever been seriously dealt with. He knows all, and can do all. His opinions and methods are as countless as the many items in a grocery store. Such a person is basically unqualified to be an authority, because the basic requirement for being God's delegated authority is to entertain no thought or opinion in oneself.

3. He must constantly keep in fellowship with the Lord. Those who are God's delegated authority need to maintain close fellowship with God. There must be not only communication but also communion.

Anyone who offers opinions freely and speaks in the name of the Lord carelessly is far away from God. He who mentions God's name casually only proves his remoteness from God. Those who are near to God have a godly fear; they know how defiling it is to carelessly express their own opinions.

Communion, therefore, is another principal requirement for one in authority. The nearer one is to the Lord, the clearer he sees his own faults. Having been brought face to face with God, he dare not thereafter speak with such firmness. He has no confidence in his flesh; he begins to be afraid lest he err. On the other hand, those who speak casually expose themselves as being far from God.

The fear of God cannot be put on outwardly; only those who

always wait on the Lord possess this virtue. Although she had heard much, it was not until the Queen of Sheba actually came into the presence of Solomon that there was no more spirit in her. But we have a greater than Solomon before us. We should be breathless, waiting at the door like servants, acknowledging that indeed we know nothing. Nothing is more serious than that a servant of God should speak carelessly before he knows the will of God. What trouble one creates when he makes a judgment before he is clear concerning the Lord's will!

"Jesus therefore answered and said unto them, Verily, verily, I say unto you, The Son can do nothing of himself, but what he seeth the Father doing: for what things soever he doeth, these the Son also doeth in like manner . . . I can of myself do nothing: as I hear, I judge: and my judgment is righteous; because I seek not mine own will, but the will of him that sent me" (John 5.19,30). In like manner should we too learn to listen, to know, and to understand. This can come only through intimate fellowship with the Lord. Only those who live in God's presence and learn of Him are qualified to speak before the brothers and sisters. They alone know what to do when there are difficulties among the brethren or problems in the church.

May I speak frankly, that the difficulty today is that many of God's servants are either too bold or too strict or too over-bearing. They dare speak what they have not heard from God! But with what authority do you thus speak? Who grants you the authority? What makes you any different from other brothers and sisters? What authority do you have if you are not sure that what you say is God's word?

Authority is representative in nature, not inherent. It means that one must live before God, learning, and being wounded so as not to project oneself into it. One should never be so mistaken as to consider oneself the authority. God alone has authority; no one else possesses it. When God's authority flows to me, it can then flow through me to others. What makes me different from others is God, not myself.

Hence we must learn to fear God and refrain from doing

anything carelessly. We should confess that we are no different from other brothers and sisters. Since God has so arranged that today I should learn to be His delegated authority, I must live in His presence, commune with Him continuously and seek to know His mind. Unless I have seen something there with God, I have nothing to say here to men.

Why do we use the word "communion"? Because we must live in the presence of the Lord continuously, not just once in awhile. Whenever we wander astray from God the character of our authority changes. May the Lord be merciful to us that we may forever live before God and fear Him.

These are the three principal requirements of a delegated authority. Since authority is of God, we have none of it within us; we are but representatives. Since authority is not ours we should not be subjective in our attitude. And since authority comes from God we must live in communion with Him. If communion is cut off, authority also ceases.

Never Try to Establish One's Own Authority

Authority is established by God; therefore no delegated authority need try to secure his authority. Do not insist that others listen to you. If they err, let them err; if they do not submit, let them be insubordinate; if they insist on going their own way, let them go. A delegated authority ought not strive with men. Why should I demand a hearing if I am not God's established authority? On the other hand, if I *am* set up by God, need I fear lest men not submit? Whoever refuses to hear me, disobeys God. It is not needful for me to force people to listen. God is my support, why then should I fear? We should never say so much as one word on behalf of our authority; rather, let us give people their liberty. The more God entrusts to us, the more liberty we grant to people. Those who are thirsty after the Lord will come to us. It is most defiling to speak on behalf of our own authority or to try to establish authority ourselves.

Although David was anointed by God and appointed to be king, for many years he remained under the hand of Saul. He did not stretch out his hand to institute his own authority. In the same way, if God ever appoints you to be an authority you too should be able to bear the opposition of others. But if you are not one who is ordained by God, any effort you make to establish authority will be painfully futile.

I do not like to hear some husbands say to their wives, "I am God's established authority; therefore you must listen to me"; nor do I take any pleasure in hearing the elders of the church say to brothers and sisters, "I am God's appointed authority." Beloved, never try to set up your own authority. If God chooses you, receive it with humility; if God does not call you, why should you strive?

Any attempt to set up oneself as an authority must be totally eradicated from among us. Let God establish His authority; let no man ever try. Should God really appoint you to be an authority, you have two alternatives before you: either you disobey and recede spiritually or you obey and receive grace.

When delegated authority entrusted to you is being tested, do nothing. Do not be in haste, nor strive, nor speak for yourself. They rebel not against you, but against God. They sin against God's authority, not against your authority. The One whom they thus disgrace, criticize, and oppose is not you. If your authority is really of God, those who oppose will find their spiritual course blocked; there will be no more revelation to them. The government of God is a most serious matter! May God be gracious to us that we may know what authority is, fearing God and distrusting ourselves!

13 Primary Credential for Delegated Authorities: Revelation

Now Moses was keeping the flock of Jethro his father-in-law, the priest of Midian: and he led the flock to the back of the wilderness, and came to the mountain of God, unto Horeb. And the angel of Jehovah appeared unto him in a flame of fire out of the midst of a bush: and he looked, and, behold, the bush burned with fire, and the bush was not consumed. And Moses said, I will turn aside now, and see this great sight, why the bush is not burnt. And when Jehovah saw that he turned aside to see, God called unto him out of the midst of the bush, and said, Moses, Moses. And he said, Here am I. And he said, Draw not nigh hither: put off thy shoes from off thy feet, for the place whereon thou standest is holy ground. Moreover he said, I am the God of thy father, the God of Abraham, the God of Isaac, and the God of Jacob. And Moses hid his face for he was afraid to look upon God. And Jehovah said, I have surely seen the affliction of my people that are in Egypt, and have heard their cry by reason of their taskmasters, for I know their sorrows; and I am come down to deliver them out of the hand of the Egyptians, and to bring them up out of that land unto a good land and a large, unto a land flowing with milk and honey; unto the place of the Canaanite, and the Hittite, and the Amorite, and the Perizzite, and the Hivite, and the Jebusite. And now, behold, the cry of the children of Israel is come unto me: moreover I have seen the oppression wherewith the Egyptians oppress them. Come now therefore, and I will send thee unto Pharaoh, that thou mayest bring forth my people

the children of Israel out of Egypt. And Moses said unto
God, Who am I, that I should go unto Pharaoh, and that I
should bring forth the children of Israel out of Egypt? And
he said, Certainly I will be with thee; and this shall be the
token unto thee, that I have sent thee: when thou hast
brought forth the people out of Egypt, ye shall serve God
upon this mountain. (Ex. 3.1-12)

And Miriam and Aaron spake against Moses because of
the Cushite woman whom he had married; for he had
married a Cushite woman. And they said, Hath Jehovah
indeed spoken only with Moses? hath he not spoken also
with us? And Jehovah heard it. Now the man Moses was very
meek, above all the men that were upon the face of the
earth.

And Jehovah spake suddenly unto Moses, and unto
Aaron, and unto Miriam, Come out ye three unto the tent of
meeting. And the three came out. And Jehovah came down
in a pillar of cloud, and stood at the door of the Tent, and
called Aaron and Miriam; and they both came forth. And he
said, Hear now my words: if there be a prophet among you, I
Jehovah will make myself known unto him in a vision, I will
speak with him in a dream. My servant Moses is not so; he is
faithful in all my house: with him will I speak mouth to
mouth, even manifestly, and not in dark speeches; and the
form of Jehovah shall he behold: wherefore then were ye not
afraid to speak against my servant, against Moses?

And the anger of Jehovah was kindled against them; and
he departed. And the cloud removed from over the Tent;
and, behold, Miriam was leprous, as white as snow: and
Aaron looked upon Miriam, and behold, she was leprous.
And Aaron said unto Moses, Oh, my lord, lay not, I pray
thee, sin upon us, for that we have done foolishly, and for
that we have sinned. Let her not, I pray, be as one dead, of
whom the flesh is half consumed when he cometh out of his
mother's womb. And Moses cried unto Jehovah, saying, Heal
her, O God, I beseech thee. And Jehovah said unto Moses, If

> her father had but spit in her face, should she not be
> ashamed seven days? let her be shut up without the camp seven
> days, and after that she shall be brought in again. And Miriam
> was shut up without the camp seven days: and the people
> journeyed not till Miriam was brought in again. (Num. 12)

No delegated authority given by God in the Old Testament was greater than that of Moses, consequently we may use him as an example from which to learn. For the time being we will pass over all the dealings he received from God and focus on how he reacted when his authority was transgressed, ridiculed, opposed, and rejected.

Before the time of his appointment by God to authority Moses had killed an Egyptian and had reprimanded the Hebrews for struggling together. When he was then challenged by a Hebrew ("Who made you a prince and a judge over us?"), Moses cracked and fled. At that time he had not yet experienced the cross and resurrection; he did everything by his natural strength. Though he was quick to reprimand and even brave to kill, within he was weak and empty. He could not stand under testing. When tried, he grew afraid and fled to the wilderness of Midian.

There, for forty years, he learned his lessons. After that long period of trials, God gave him one day a vision of the burning bush. The bush was on fire, yet it was not consumed. With this vision, God appointed him to authority. Let us now skip ahead to notice how Moses reacted later on when his brother Aaron and sister Miriam spoke against him and rejected his delegated authority.

Do Not Listen to Slanderous Words

They questioned Moses: Do you alone speak for God—you who have married a Cushite woman? Has not God spoken through us also? How can a seed of Shem married to a seed of Ham continue in God's ministry? Can we not minister, we who are children of Shem and not married to children of Ham? Of all this, the Bible simply records, "And Jehovah heard it." It was as if Moses had never heard it. Hence we find a man who could not be touched by men's words, for he was beyond the reach of slanderous words.

All who desire to be God's spokesmen and desire to help the brothers and sisters must learn not to listen to slanders. Let God do the listening. On your part, do not pay any attention to how people criticize you; do not get angry because of others' words. Those who are disturbed and overwhelmed by words of slander prove themselves unfit to be a delegated authority.

Make No Self Defense

Vindication or defense or whatever reaction there may be should come from God, not from man. He who vindicates himself does not know God. No one on earth could ever be more authoritative than Christ, yet He never defended Himself. Authority and self-defense are incompatible. The one against whom you defend yourself becomes your judge. He rises higher than you when you begin to answer his criticism. He who speaks for himself is under judgment; therefore he is without authority. Whenever one tries to justify himself, he loses authority.

Paul stood before the Corinthian believers as a delegated authority, yet he said: "I judge not mine own self" (1 Cor. 4.3). Vindication comes from God. The moment you justify yourself before a person, he becomes your judge. As soon as you try to explain, you are fallen before him.

Very Meek

Verse 2 of Numbers 12 records that God heard the slander, and verse 4, that God took action. But in between comes verse 3 as a parenthetic statement: "Now the man Moses was very meek, above all the men that were upon the face of the earth." Moses did not strive, because he realized he had erred. God cannot appoint a stiff-necked person to authority; He will not delegate authority to an arrogant person. Those whom He sets up in authority are the meek and the tender—and this is not ordinary meekness, it is the meekness of God.

We should never try to establish our own authority. The more we try, the less are we fit for authority. It is not the violent or the strong but a man like Paul—whose bodily presence is weak and whose speech is of no account—whom God will establish as authority. The Lord said that His kingdom is not of this world and that therefore His servants need not fight for Him. Authority attained through fighting is not what is given by God.

People usually assume such things as the following to be the necessary requirements for an authority: splendor and magnificence; strength of personality, bearing or appearance; and power. To be an authority, they reason, one must possess a strong determination, clever ideas, and eloquent lips. But it is not these that represent authority; instead they stand for the flesh.

No one in the Old Testament exceeded Moses as a God-established authority, yet he was the meekest of all men. While he was in Egypt he was quite fierce, both in killing the Egyptian and in reprimanding the Hebrews. He dealt with people by his own fleshly hand. So at that time God did not appoint him as an authority. It was only after he had passed through many trials and been dealt with by God, only after he had become very meek—more than all men on earth—that God used him to be an authority. The person least likely to be given authority is often the very one who considers himself an authority. Likewise, the more authority a person thinks he has, the less he actually does have.

Revelation: the One Credential of Authority

"And Jehovah spake suddenly unto Moses, and unto Aaron, and unto Miriam, Come out ye three unto the tent of meeting."

"Suddenly" means "unexpectedly." Aaron and Miriam may have spoken against Moses many times, but now abruptly God called the three of them to the tent of meeting. Many who rebel against authority do so outside the tent. It is very easy and convenient to criticize at home; even so, everything will be cleared up in the tent of meeting. As the three came to the tent the Lord spoke to Aaron and Miriam, "Hear now my words." In the past they had murmured, "Hath Jehovah indeed spoken only with Moses?" Now the Lord asked them to come and hear His words, revealing the fact that they had never before heard God's words. Aaron and Miriam had never known what God was saying. This was the first time the Lord spoke to them—and it was not in revelation but in reproof, not the manifestation of God's glory but the judgment of their conduct.

"Hear *now* my words" means that not only had the Lord not spoken before but that furthermore He was indicating that He wanted to be allowed to speak this once since they had already been speaking for so many days. "You who are well able to speak, hear now My words!" From this we can safely conclude that the talkative are not able to hear God's word; only the meek can do so. Moses was one who did not talk but did as he was told. It made no difference to him whether he advanced or retreated as long as it was of God. Aaron and Miriam, however, were different; they were hard and obstinate. Thus God even said: "If there be a prophet among you," as though He had forgotten that they were prophets.

Though Aaron and Miriam were prophets, the Lord only made Himself known to them in dreams and visions. With Moses it was not so, because God spoke mouth to mouth with him, clearly, and not in dark speech. Such was God's vindication. The revelation was given to Moses, not to Aaron and Miriam; for it is those who meet God face to face whom God establishes as authority. To set up authority belongs to God's jurisdiction; man is not allowed to intrude, nor can man's slander repudiate any authority. It was God who established Moses and God alone who could reject him. This was God's business; no person should interfere, therefore, with what God has established.

A man's value before God is not decided by others' judgment nor by his own judgment. He is measured by the revelation he receives from God. Revelation is God's valuation and measurement. Authority is built on God's revelation, and His estimation of a person is according to that revelation. If God gives revelation, authority is established; but when His revelation is withdrawn, the man is rejected.

If we want to learn to be an authority we must pay attention to what is our state before God. If God is willing to give us revelation and to speak clearly with us, if we have face-to-face communion with Him, then no one can eliminate us. But if our communication above is severed and the heavens are shut, and though we were fully prospered on this earth, it will all come to naught. An open heaven is the seal of God and the testimony of sonship. After the Lord Jesus was baptized, the heavens opened to Him. Baptism symbolizes death. It was at the time when he entered into death and the greatest suffering, when it was all dark and there was no way out, that the heavens opened.

Revelation is therefore the evidence of authority. We must learn not to strive or to speak for ourselves. We should not join the ranks of Aaron and Miriam in struggling for authority. Indeed, if we do strive, it only proves that our authority is wholly carnal, dark, and void of heavenly vision.

Moses "is faithful in all my house" (Num. 12.7). Moses, a type of Christ, was faithful in the house of Israel. God called him "My servant." To be God's servant simply means that I belong to God, I am His possession, I have been sold to Him, and I have thereby lost my freedom. This explains why God cannot remain quiet but speaks out when His servants are slandered. We have no need to vindicate ourselves. What good is it for me to speak if God does not step forward to do it? Why should any of us try to reinforce our authority? If our authority is from God we need not strengthen it. Revelation shall be the proof. If there are those who speak against us let God turn off His supply and seal up His revelation to them, thus proving that we are appointed by Him.

Whoever offends God's delegated authorities offends the One whom they represent. If they are the Lord's, they shall find a closed heaven above them, and they will have to humbly acknowledge those authorities whom God has established. Therefore, no one needs to strengthen his own authority; everything depends on God's proof. By shutting away revelation from others God proves to them whom He has appointed as His delegated authority.

No Personal Feeling

"Wherefore then were ye not afraid to speak against my servant, against Moses?" asked God. To Him, such slander was simply terrible. God, being God, knows what is love, what is light, and what is glory. But does He know what is fear? No doubt He does, because here He was fearful for Aaron and Miriam. As God, He has nothing to fear; nonetheless He was telling these two persons what a terrible thing they had done. Whereupon He ceased speaking with them and left in anger. This was how God maintained *His* authority, not Moses' authority. He did not say, Why did you speak against Moses; rather, Why did you speak against My servant Moses. He would not suffer anyone to impair His authority. If His authority is challenged, He will leave in anger. Thus the cloud, representing the presence of God, removed from the tent; and behold, Miriam was leprous. Aaron saw it and was afraid, for he too had a part in the rebellion, though Miriam no doubt had taken the lead.

The tent refused to give revelation, and Moses opened not his mouth. Although Moses was an eloquent man, he kept silent. Those who do not know how to control their hearts and lips are not fit to be authorities. But when Aaron pleaded with Moses, the latter cried to the Lord. During the entire affair Moses acted as though he were nothing more than a spectator. He had no personal ax to grind; he neither murmured nor reproved. He had no personal feeling, no opinion of his own. He had no intention to judge or to punish. But as soon as God's purpose was accomplished, he quickly forgave.

Authority is set up to execute God's order, not to uplift oneself. It is to give God's children a sense of God, not to give a sense of oneself. The important thing is to help people to be subject to God's authority; it was therefore a small matter to Moses if he were rejected. So Moses cried to the Lord, "Heal her, O God, I beseech thee." Let us too be delivered from personal feeling, for the presence of it will damage God's affairs and bind God's hand.

Had Moses not known God's grace, then he certainly would have said to Aaron, "Why do you not yourself pray to God since you insist God speaks to you also?" And Moses would have also said to God, "Vindicate me, or I shall resign my post!" But Moses neither defended himself nor sought revenge on Aaron and Miriam, nor took advantage of God's vindication. He had no personal feeling, because he did not live in himself. His natural life had been dealt with; and thus he so readily pleaded for Miriam's recovery. His action was like that of Christ's when He asked God to forgive those who crucified Him.

Hence Moses proved himself to be God's delegated authority, for he was one able to represent God. He was not touched by the natural life, nor did he protect himself by seeking defense or revenge. God's authority could be diffused through him without any hindrance. Indeed, people met God's authority in him. To be a delegated authority is not at all an easy thing, because it requires the emptying of oneself.

The Character of Delegated Authorities: Graciousness

Moses' First Reaction towards Rebellion—Falling on His Face

There can be no rebellion on the part of the Israelites more serious than that which is recorded in Numbers Chapter 16. The leader of the rebellion was Korah, son of Levi, joined by Dathan and Abiram, sons of Reuben, and supported by two hundred and fifty leaders of the congregation. They assembled themselves together and with strong words attacked Moses and Aaron (verse 3). The slander of Numbers 12 was only on the part of Aaron and Miriam, and even then it was more hidden. But here the rebellion was a collective thing and the attack upon Moses and Aaron was open and direct. So let us in this situation pay special attention to: (1) What was Moses' personal state and attitude? and (2) How did Moses react to the crisis, how did he answer the rebellious ones?

Moses' first reaction was, that "he fell upon his face" (verse 4). This is verily the attitude every servant of God should have. The people were excited and so many were speaking, but Moses alone was prostrating himself upon the ground. Here again we are confronted by one who knows authority. Being truly gentle, he was empty of personal feeling. He neither defended himself nor got stirred up. The first thing he did was to fall on his face. Then he told them: "Jehovah will show who are his, and who is holy, and will cause him to come near unto him: even him whom he shall choose will he cause to come near unto him" (verse 5). It was not necessary to strive. Moses did not dare say anything for himself, because he knew the Lord would show who was His. It would be better to let God do the distinguishing. Moses had faith and thus he dared to trust everything to God. The Lord would give His judgment the next morning when they all came before Him with incense. Moses' words were meek yet weighty. "Ye take too much upon you, ye sons of Levi," was the sigh of an old man who well knew God (verse 7).

Exhortation and Restoration

Moses exhorted Korah with words so as to restore him. He knew the seriousness of this matter and was really concerned for the rebellious ones. He not only sighed but exhorted them as well, saying,

> Hear now, ye sons of Levi: seemeth it but a small thing unto you, that the God of Israel hath separated you from the congregation of Israel to bring you near to himself, to do the service of the tabernacle of Jehovah, and to stand before the congregation to minister unto them . . . And seek ye the priesthood also? Therefore thou and all thy company are gathered together against Jehovah: and Aaron, what is he that ye murmur against him?" (verses 8-11)

Exhortation is not an expression of lordliness; rather does it disclose meekness. He who persuades in return to attack is truly a meek person. But he who allows people to be in the wrong without any intention of restoring them proves his heart to be hard. To not exhort at such a time would be due to a lack of humility; it would obviously suggest pride. Moses was willing to exhort when attacked and then afterwards he gave his slanderers a whole night's time to repent.

Moses dealt with the rebellious ones separately. He first dealt with the Levite, Korah, then with Dathan and Abiram. He sent someone to call Dathan and Abiram to come, but they refused, clearly indicating they had broken with Moses (verse 12). In

Moses' action we can see that those who represent authority seek for restoration, not division, even after they have been rejected. Those rebellious men accused Moses of bringing them out of a land flowing with milk and honey (verse 13). How absurd was the accusation. Already they had forgotten that instead of milk and honey in Egypt they had been forced to make bricks and sometimes even without the supply of straw. These rebellious ones were no different from the ten spies who, after having clearly seen the abundance of Canaan, refused to enter in, yet blamed Moses for it. Their rebellion had reached the point of no return. There was nothing left but judgment. Hence Moses grew very angry and went to the Lord for a showdown (verse 15).

God came out to judge. He would consume not only Korah who was the chief instigator but also the congregation who followed Korah. But Moses fell on his face and pleaded for the congregation (verse 22). God answered his prayer and spared the congregation but ordered them to depart from the tents of the wicked. Then He judged Korah, Dathan, and Abiram.

No Judging Spirit

While God was preparing to mete out judgment to the rebellious, Moses clearly said that "Jehovah hath sent me to do all these words; for I have not done them of mine own mind" (verse 28). So far as his own feeling went he had no intention of judging anyone who rebelled against him. He proved himself to be the true servant of God when he insisted that these people had not sinned against him but that they had sinned against God. Let us learn how to touch a man's spirit. We find that in Moses there was not the slightest thought of judging. He acted in obedience to God because he was God's servant. He had no personal feeling except that he felt they had sinned against God. He further explained that the Lord would prove this to them by creating something new (verse 30). Thus God executed a great judgment to establish Moses' authority. Three families were destroyed and two hundred fifty leaders were burned to death (verses 27-35). The way of the rebellious leads to Sheol; rebellion and death are joined together. Authority is something which God establishes; all who offend His established authorities despise God. But in Moses we find a delegated authority who had neither his own opinion nor a judging spirit.

Intercession and Atonement

Although the whole congregation of Israel witnessed the opening of the earth and the swallowing up of the rebellious families, and although they fled in terror, their fear was only of the punishment, not at all of God. They failed to understand Moses; their hearts remained untouched. So that after a night's thought, they themselves rebelled the very next day (verse 41). Unless one has met the grace of God, his inward condition remains the same.

The entire congregation murmured against Moses and Aaron, declaring: "Ye have killed the people of Jehovah" (verse 41). Let us notice now the whole story of how these delegated authorities responded to such a reaction against them.

Humanly speaking, Moses should be very angry at the attack. Clearly what had been done was God's doing; why should they murmur against him? Why did they not murmur against God rather than turn against His delegated authority? But God's reaction came more swiftly than Moses and Aaron's. Behold, the cloud covered the tent, and the glory of the Lord appeared (verse 42). God came to judge the congregation, and so He told Moses and Aaron to get away from the midst of the people. It was as though God were saying to Moses and Aaron: your prayer of yesterday was a mistake, today I am going to annihilate the whole congregation.

Nevertheless Moses and Aaron fell on their faces for the third time (verse 45). Moses' spiritual sense was so keen that he knew immediately this problem could not be solved by prayer alone.

The sin of yesterday was not as open as the sin of today. He quickly told Aaron to take his censer, go to the congregation, and make atonement for them (verse 46). Moses was certainly fit to be a delegated authority. He knew what a tragic consequence could come upon the people of Israel, and he was still hoping that God would be gracious to forgive. His heart was full of love and compassion, the yearning of one who truly knows God. Moses was not a priest, hence he requested Aaron to quickly atone for the people. Here was intercession plus atonement. The plague had already begun among the people; Aaron now stood between the dead and the living; with the result that the plague was stopped. Now those who died by the plague were fourteen thousand seven hundred (verse 49). Had Moses and Aaron been less alert, surely many more would have died.

The atoning grace seen in Moses was astonishingly similar to that seen in his Lord. He cared for God's people and he bore the responsibilities of both the obedient and the rebellious. A person who cares only for himself and who often complains of the responsibility he bears for others is unfit to represent authority. The way one reacts proves the type of person he is. Many think only of saving their faces and are extremely sensitive to the criticisms of others. All their thoughts are self-centered. Moses, however, was faithful in all the house of God. Possibly if God's house had suffered, Moses' flesh would have been satisfied; but he would not have been a faithful servant. A faithful servant, though personally rejected and despised himself, will bear the burdens of many. The Israelites rebelled against Moses, yet Moses bore their sins; they opposed and rejected him, yet he still interceded for them. If we care only for our own feelings we will not be able to bear the problems of God's children.

Let us therefore confess our sin, acknowledging that we are just too small and too hard. God's desire for us is that we have grace within. May we be those who allow God to judge in all things. To be gracious to others is the character of all who are in authority.

15 | The Basis for Being Delegated Authorities: Resurrection

And Jehovah spake unto Moses, saying, Speak unto the children of Israel, and take of them rods, one for each fathers' house, of all their princes according to their fathers' houses, twelve rods: write thou every man's name upon his rod. And thou shalt write Aaron's name upon the rod of Levi; for there shall be one rod for each head of their fathers' houses. And thou shalt lay them up in the tent of meeting before the testimony, where I meet with you. And it shall come to pass, that the rod of the man whom I shall choose shall bud: and I will make to cease from me the murmurings of the children of Israel, which they murmur against you. And Moses spake unto the children of Israel; and all their princes gave him rods, for each prince one, according to their fathers' houses, even twelve rods: and the rod of Aaron was among their rods. And Moses laid up the rods before Jehovah in the tent of the testimony.

And it came to pass on the morrow, that Moses went into the tent of the testimony; and, behold, the rod of Aaron for the house of Levi was budded, and put forth buds, and produced blossoms, and bare ripe almonds. And Moses brought out all the rods from before Jehovah unto all the children of Israel: and they looked, and took every man his rod. And Jehovah said unto Moses, Put back the rod of Aaron before the testimony, to be kept for a token against the children of rebellion; that thou mayest make an end of their murmurings against me, that they die not. Thus did Moses: as Jehovah commanded him, so did he. (Num. 17.1-11)

The purpose of the incident in Numbers 17 is to deal with the rebellion of the people of Israel. In the preceding chapter we witnessed a rebellion exceeding all others; in the chapter before us now we are to see how God puts an end to such rebellion by delivering His people both from it and its consequence, death. God will prove to Israel that the authorities came from Him and that He had a basis and a reason for establishing them. Every person to whom God grants authority must have this basic experience. Otherwise he cannot be appointed by God.

Resurrection Life Is Basis of Authority

God commanded the twelve tribal leaders to get twelve rods, one for each father's house, and put them in the tent of meeting before the testimony. The rod of the man whom God chose would sprout. A rod is a piece of wood, a branch of tree, cut on both ends. It is cleared of leaves on one end and of roots on the other. Once it was alive but now it is dead. Formerly it drew sap from the tree and was able to bloom and bear fruit, but now it is a dead rod. All twelve were stripped of leaves and roots, all were dead and dried. But God said if one should sprout, it would be the rod of the one whom He had chosen. This suggests that resurrection is the basis for election as well as for authority.

In Chapter 16 the people rebelled against God's appointed authority; in Chapter 17 God confirms the authority He had appointed. God verified that the basis for authority was resurrection, thus putting an end to all the murmurings of the people. The people had no right to ask for God's reason, nonetheless God condescended Himself to inform them what His basis for His establishing of authorities was. The basis was resurrection; this was something the people of Israel could not argue about.

Naturally, both Aaron and the Israelites came from Adam. Both were children of wrath according to natural life; there was no difference. These twelve rods were all the same, all stripped of leaves and roots, dead and lifeless. The basis of ministry lies in being given resurrection life apart from the natural life. And *this* constitutes authority. Authority depends not on the person but on resurrection. Aaron was not different from the others except that God had chosen him and given him a resurrection life.

Sprouting of the Dried Rod Keeps Men Humble

It is God who makes a rod sprout. It is He who puts the power of life into a dead and dried rod. The rod which sprouts causes both the owner of that rod to be humble and the murmurings of the owners of other rods to cease. The rod that we originally take is as dried and dead and hopeless as Aaron's, but if it sprouts and blooms and bears fruit on the second day we ought to weep before God and say, "This is your doing; it has nothing to do with me; this is your glory, not mine." We will naturally be humbled before God, for it is truly the treasure in the earthen vessel, demonstrating that the transcendent power belongs to God and not to us. Only the foolish can be proud. Those who are favored will prostrate themselves before God, saying, "This has been done by God; there is nothing of which man can boast; it is all of God's mercy, not of man's running. What is there that has not been received, for it is all of God's choosing?"

Let us accordingly realize that authority is not based upon us. In fact, it has no relation to us. Hereafter whenever Aaron used his authority in ministering to God he could confess, "My rod is just as dead as the others. The only reason I can serve and they cannot, why I have spiritual authority and they do not, is not in the rods (for all are equally dried), but due to God's mercy and choice." Aaron did not serve in the power of the rod, but in the power of the sprouting of the rod.

Touchstone of Ministry Is Resurrection

The rod indicates man's position, but sprouting indicates

resurrection life. As far as position was concerned, those twelve men were all in the position of leadership in the twelve tribes of Israel. Aaron merely represented the tribe of Levi, one of the twelve tribes. He could not serve God on the ground of his position, for the other tribes would not agree to it. How did God solve the problem? He ordered them to deposit twelve rods—one each—in the tent of meeting before the testimony. The rods were to stay there throughout the night, and the rod of the man whom He chose would sprout.

This is life out of death. Only those who have passed through death and come out in resurrection are recognized by God as His servants. The touchstone of ministry is resurrection. No one may point to his position; it must be of God's choice. After God made Aaron's rod sprout, bud, and bear fruit, and the other leaders had all seen it, they had nothing more to say.

Authority, then, does not come by striving. It is set up by God. It depends not on a position of leadership but on the experience of death and resurrection. Men are chosen to exercise spiritual authority not because they are different from the rest but on the basis of grace, election, and resurrection. It requires great darkness and blindness to be proud! As far as we are concerned, though we might deposit our rods for a lifetime they would still not sprout. The difficulty in this present day is that so few fall on their faces acknowledging that they are no different from the others.

The Foolish Are Proud

When the Lord Jesus entered Jerusalem riding on a colt the crowds shouted, "Hosanna to the Son of David: Blessed is he that cometh in the name of the Lord; Hosanna in the highest" (Matt. 21.9). Let us suppose for a moment that the colt, upon hearing the cry of hosanna and seeing the branches on the road, should turn to the Lord and ask, "Is this cry for you or for me?", or should turn to the ass and say, "After all, I am nobler than you." It would be evident that the colt did not recognize the One who rode upon It.

Many of God's servants are just as foolish. There was no difference between the ass and the colt; it is the Lord on the colt who was to be praised. The shouts of hosanna are not for you; neither are the branches spread for you. Only a fool would say, "I am better than you." When Aaron first saw his rod sprouted, his immediate reaction would be a sense of wonder. He would fall on his face and worship, saying, "How is it that my rod has sprouted? Is not my rod the same as the other rods? Why does God grant me such glory and power? By myself I can never sprout. That which is born of the flesh is flesh. As the people of God are, so am I." Others might be confused, but Aaron was clear. He knew that all his spiritual authority had been given by God. None of us has a right to be proud.

If we receive mercy today, it is because God has been willing. Who is competent for this ministry? Our competency is of God. For one to live in the presence of God and not be humble would be most strange. It would take a tremendous amount of self-confidence and foolishness on the part of the colt to imagine that the praise of that day was directed to it. One day it would wake up and be ashamed of itself. True, we shall be glorified, but our glory lies in the future, not now.

Young brothers and sisters should learn the lesson of humility. We all need to know that it does not in the least depend on us to run the course ahead. We should not consider ourselves different from others just because we have learned a little of spiritual lessons. All is God's grace, all is given by God, nothing comes from ourselves.

Aaron knew well that it was God who made his rod sprout, because the sprouting had been effected through supernatural power. God used this means to speak to Aaron as well as to the people of Israel. Hereafter Aaron knew that all ministry was based on sprouting, not on himself. Today as we minister before God we too ought to know that ministry comes from resurrection and resurrection comes from God.

What Is Resurrection?

Resurrection means that which is not of the natural, not of self or self-capability. It is what I cannot do, for it is beyond my ability. I can paint color and carve flowers on the rod, but I cannot make it sprout. No one has ever heard of an old rod sprouting, nor a woman in old age conceiving. Sarah gave birth to Isaac: this was God's doing. Hence Sarah represents resurrection. Resurrection is that which I cannot, but which God can; what I am not, but what God is. It matters not what I am, for it is based on God. It does not depend on greater cleverness or better eloquence. Whatever I have of spirituality is due to God's own working on me.

How absurd and foolish Aaron would be if he insisted that his rod sprouted because it was different from the other rods, more polished and straighter. If for one moment we think of ourselves as being better than others, we have done the most foolish thing in the world. Whatever difference there is comes from the Lord.

Isaac means laughter. Sarah laughed because she knew she was too old to conceive. She considered it impossible. Thus God called her child Isaac. In serving the Lord, we too should laugh and say: I cannot, I know for sure that I am unable, but this is the doing of the Lord. If there is any manifestation of authority, we must confess that it is His doing, not ours.

Resurrection Is Permanent Rule for Service

God returned all the rods to their respective owners except Aaron's rod which had sprouted. It was to remain in the ark for an everlasting memorial. This suggests that resurrection is the permanent rule for service. Unless a service passes through death into resurrection, it is not accepted by God. What is risen again is of God; it is not of us. All who reckon themselves as commendable have no knowledge of what resurrection is. Those who know resurrection have already despaired of themselves. So long as natural strength remains, the power of resurrection is obscured.

God's greatest power is not manifested in creation; it is shown in resurrection. Whatever man is capable of is not of resurrection. We must come to a place where we count ourselves as nothing, even as dead dogs; we must be so completely undone that all we can say to God is: "Whatever there is, is given by You: anything which has been done, has been all of You. Hereafter I will no more be mistaken about this, for I am fully persuaded that whatsoever is dead comes from me, but anything alive is of You." Thus ought we to be aware of this distinction. The lord never misunderstands, yet we often misinterpret. It was absolutely impossible for Sarah to imagine that Isaac had been born through her strength. God must lead us to the point where we will never misunderstand God's doing.

Authority is of God, not of us. We are merely stewards of His authority. Such an insight makes us fit to be delegated authorities. Whenever we attempt to exercise authority as if it were our own, we are immediately dispossessed of any authority whatsoever. The dried rod can only dispense death. Where resurrection is, there is authority, because authority rests in resurrection and not in the natural. Since all we have is what is natural, we have no authority except in the Lord.

What Paul says in 2 Corinthians 4.7 harmonizes with the above interpretation. He compares himself to an earthen vessel, and the treasure, to the power of resurrection. He realizes quite well that he is merely an earthen vessel, but that the treasure in him possesses transcendent power. As to himself, he is afflicted in every way; yet through the treasure he is not crushed. There is death on the one hand, but life on the other. He is always given up to death, yet at the same time he manifests life. Where death is working, there life is manifested. We find the center of Paul's ministry in 2 Corinthians Chapters 4 and 5; and the rule of his ministry is death and resurrection. What is in us is death; what is in the Lord is resurrection.

Let us make no mistake that authority is of God. Each of us must clearly understand that all authority belongs to the Lord. We merely maintain the Lord's authority on earth, but we ourselves are not authority. Whenever we depend on the Lord we have authority. But as soon as a little of the natural comes in, we are as others—without authority. All that is of resurrection has authority. Authority comes from resurrection and not from ourselves. It is more than simply depositing the rod before God; it is the rod of resurrection which remains in the presence of God. To be God's delegated authority is not merely to manifest a little of resurrection, but it is to have the rod sprout, bloom, and bear fruit, thus becoming matured resurrection life.

16 Misuse of Authority and God's Governmental Discipline

And there was no water for the congregation; and they assembled themselves together against Moses and against Aaron. And the people strove with Moses, and spake, saying, Would that we had died when our brethren died before Jehovah! ... And Jehovah spake unto Moses, saying, Take the rod, and assemble the congregation, thou, and Aaron thy brother, and speak ye unto the rock before their eyes, that it give forth its water; and thou shalt bring forth to them water out of the rock; so thou shalt give the congregation and their cattle drink. And Moses took the rod from before Jehovah, as he commanded him.

And Moses and Aaron gathered the assembly together before the rock, and he said unto them, Hear now, ye rebels; shall we bring you forth water out of this rock? And Moses lifted up his hand, and smote the rock with his rod twice: and water came forth abundantly, and the congregation drank, and their cattle. And Jehovah said unto Moses and Aaron, Because ye believed not in me, to sanctify me in the eyes of the children of Israel, therefore ye shall not bring this assembly into the land which I have given them. These are the waters of Meribah; because the children of Israel strove with Jehovah, and he was sanctified in them. (Num. 20.2-3, 7-13)

And Jehovah spake unto Moses and Aaron in mount Hor, by the border of the land of Edom, saying, Aaron shall be gathered unto his people; for he shall not enter into the land which I have given unto the children of Israel, because ye rebelled against my word at the waters of Meribah. Take Aaron and Eleazar his son, and bring them up unto mount

Hor; and strip Aaron of his garments, and put them upon
Eleazar his son: and Aaron shall be gathered unto his people,
and shall die there. And Moses did as Jehovah commanded:
and they went up into mount Hor in the sight of all the
congregation. And Moses stripped Aaron of his garments, and
put them upon Eleazar his son; and Aaron died there on the
top of the mount: and Moses and Eleazar came down from
the mount. (Num. 20.23-28)

And Jehovah spake unto Moses that selfsame day, saying,
Get thee up into this mountain of Abarim, unto mount
Nebo, which is in the land of Moab, that is over against
Jericho; and behold the land of Canaan, which I give unto
the children of Israel for a possession; and die in the mount
whither thou goest up, and be gathered unto thy people, as
Aaron thy brother died in mount Hor, and was gathered unto
his people: because ye trespassed against me in the midst of
the children of Israel at the waters of Meribah of Kadesh, in
the wilderness of Zin; because ye sanctified me not in the
midst of the children of Israel. For thou shalt see the land
before thee; but thou shalt not go thither into the land which
I give the children of Israel. (Deut. 32.48-52)

Delegated Authority Ought to Sanctify God

After over thirty years of wandering in the wilderness the
people of Israel again forgot the lessons they had learned through
their rebellion. When they came to the wilderness of Zin and
found no water they once again contended with Moses and
Aaron, uttering many unpleasant words. God nevertheless was
not angry with them. He merely commanded to take the rod and
speak to the rock that it might give water. Moses took the rod, a
symbol of God's authority, in his hands. However, he was so
provoked by anger that he called the people rebels and then,
ignoring God's command, he smote the rock twice with the rod.
He erred, yet water still flowed out of the rock.

Because of this, God reprimanded His servant, saying, "You did not believe in me, to sanctify me in the eyes of the people of Israel." It meant that Moses had not set God apart from himself and Aaron. He had misrepresented God, for it was of himself that he had had a wrong spirit and had thus spoken wrongly and smote wrongly. God seemingly remonstrated with Moses on this wise: "I saw my people thirsty and was willing to give them to drink, so why did you scold them?" God did not reprove the people, but Moses did. And so he gave the people of Israel a wrong impression about God, as though God were fierce and reviling and lacking in grace.

To be an authority is to represent God. Whether it be in wrath or mercy, an authority must always be like God. If, in such a position, we do anything wrong, we should acknowledge it as our own doing. We ought never draw God into our own fault. Because Moses misrepresented God, he had to be judged. If anyone in authority misrepresents God and does not confess it, God will have to vindicate Himself.

Thus He showed the people of Israel that this was Moses' doing, not His. True, the people had murmured and perhaps their attitude had been rebellious, nevertheless God had not judged them. How could Moses be so impatient as to judge them before God did, and to speak angrily without restraint? It was *his* attitude and *his* wrath, but most likely the people of Israel got the impression that it was God's attitude and God's wrath. Hence God had to acquit Himself by separating Himself from Moses and Aaron.

Let us be careful that we never draw God into human failure by giving the wrong impression that He is expressing His attitude through us. In case such a wrong impression is made, God will have to absolve Himself. A delegated authority is supposed to manage affairs for God. If we should become angry, let us confess that this anger comes from us and not from God. The two must be separated. It is a dreadful thing to mix up one's own doing with God's.

We are too prone to err. Accordingly, whenever we do err, let us immediately acknowledge that it is our own error. Then we will not misrepresent God and give the evil one any ground, nor will we fall into darkness. If we confess first, then God will not need to defend Himself and we shall be delivered from falling into His governmental hand.

To Be a Delegated Authority Is a Serious Matter

As a consequence of the above incident, God announced that both Moses and Aaron were not to be allowed to enter Canaan. If a person should speak carelessly and do something in a way which does not sanctify God, then, from the moment God has to step in to justify Himself there is no way left to ask for forgiveness. We must fear and tremble when we are managing the affairs of God. Let us beware lest we grow careless and reckless as we become older.

In earlier days, when Moses' anger burned hot and he smashed into pieces the tables on which God had written the law, God did not blame him. He had touched God's heart of jealousy, and so his anger was justified. Now, after having followed the Lord for many more years and yet failing to do as He commanded by smiting the rock twice and speaking hasty words, Moses had misrepresented God. For this, he was kept out of Canaan.

The people of Israel rebelled against God many times, but He was patient with them. Moses and Aaron, though, committed one mistake and yet they were barred from Canaan. It shows how serious it is to be delegated authorities. God is most strict with those who represent Him. In Numbers 18 the Lord said to Aaron, "Thou and thy sons and thy fathers' house with thee shall bear the iniquity of the sanctuary" (verse 1). The more authority which is delegated, the severer is God's dealing. The Lord also said, "To whomsoever much is given, of him shall much be required: and to whom they commit much, of him will they ask the more" (Luke 12.48).

It is truly a beautiful picture to see Moses and Aaron and Eleazar his son ascend together to Mount Hor. All of them were obedient to God in humbly accepting God's judgment. They did not even pray, for they knew God. Aaron knew his day had arrived, and Moses was also conscious of his own future. God ordered Moses to perform the transaction, since at the waters of Meribah Moses had also been the chief character. By viewing how Aaron went, it was made known to Moses how he would also go.

As Aaron was stripped of his holy garments, he died. Ordinarily people do not die by their clothes being stripped off, but Aaron did, because his life was maintained by service. This suggests that the life of one who serves God ceases when his service ends.

Many years elapsed after the above, yet God's judgment did not pass away. Eventually He dealt with Moses in the same way He had dealt with Aaron. He summoned Moses to Mount Nebo to die, even though during the intervening years Moses had remained faithful. Before his death Moses blessed the people of Israel with a song, but he did not ask to be exempted from his particular judgment (see Deut. 33). He too humbled himself under the mighty hand of God. He who had represented God's authority and who had obeyed Him all his life except in that one instance in his old age, was not permitted to enter Canaan. What tremendous loss Moses incurred. He could not partake of God's promise made to Abraham six hundred years ago!

Nothing is more serious nor regarded more severely than for a delegated authority to do wrongly. Every time we execute authority we must ask to be united with God. If a mistake is made let us swiftly separate it from God lest we incur His judgment. Before we decide anything, let us seek to know His mind. Only after ascertaining His mind may we do it in His name. Moses could not claim that what he had done at the waters of Meribah was done in the Lord's name. Let us not be foolish, but let us learn to fear and tremble before God. Do not render judgment carelessly; rather, control your spirit and your mouth, especially at the time of provocation. The more one knows God, the less he is careless. There are some times when one may receive forgiveness after having fallen into God's governmental hand, but this does not always happen. The government of God ought not be offended. Let us be clear about it.

Delegated Authorities Should Not Err

For our service to be approved by God we must not serve with our own strength but serve on resurrection ground. We ourselves have no authority, we are only representing authority. Thus the flesh has no place. We only cause problems if we do anything according to our own whims. The church is not only afraid of there being no authority, it is also afraid of the wrong authority. God has one thought, and that is to establish His own authority.

In the church submission to authority must be absolute. Without submission there can be no church. In like manner, the attitude of fear and trembling in those who represent authority must also be absolute. There are two difficulties in the church: the lack of absolute submission and the presence of wrong authority. We need to learn not to speak inadvertently, not to offer opinion carelessly. Our spirit must always be kept open towards the Lord, expecting His ready light. Otherwise, we will drag God into our error and do things in His name which are not of Him. For this reason, we must learn on the one hand how to submit and on the other hand how to represent God. This means we must know the cross and the resurrection. Whether the church has a future depends very much on how well we learn our lessons.

Authority Comes from Ministry, Ministry from Resurrection

A person's authority is based on his ministry, and his ministry is in turn based on resurrection. If there is no resurrection there can be no ministry; and if there is no ministry, there is no authority. Aaron's ministry came from resurrection; without that, he could not serve at all. God has never set up as an authority anyone who is without ministry.

Today authority is not a matter of position. Where spiritual ministry is lacking, there can be no positional authority. Whoever has spiritual service before God has authority before men. This means that one's spiritual ministry gives him authority among God's children. Who, then, can fight for this authority, for there is no way to strive for ministry? Just as ministry is distributed by the Lord, so authority is also decided by Him.

All authority is based on ministry. Aaron possessed authority because he had service before God. His censer could atone for the people and cause the plague to cease, whereas the censers of the two hundred fifty leaders were cursed by God. The rebellion in Numbers 16 was directed not only against authority but also against ministry. Aaron was in authority for he possessed ministry. No one's authority can exceed his ministry.

We should not attempt to outdo the authority of our ministry. Our attitude must always be that we dare not occupy ourselves with things too great and too marvelous for us (see Ps. 131.1). Let us learn instead to be faithful before God according to our portion. Many brothers mistakenly imagine that they can take up authority at random, not knowing that the authority which comes from ministry never lords it over God's children. One's authority before men is equal to one's ministry before God. The measure of ministry determines the proportion of authority. If authority exceeds ministry it becomes positional, and is therefore no longer spiritual.

If a delegated authority errs, God will come to judge. The highest principle in God's government is His own vindication. Since God is willing to give His name to us and allows us to use it—just as someone trusts his seal to us for us to use—then He must exonerate Himself if we misrepresent Him. He will tell the people that the fault is not His but ours.

Aaron died, and Moses died too. They were not allowed to enter Canaan. Did they strive with God? No, because they were aware that God's justification was far more important than their entry into Canaan. They would rather be barred from Canaan that God might acquit Himself. As can be seen in Deuteronomy 32, Moses took pains to explain to the people that it was Israel's fault, not God's. Hence we must maintain the absoluteness of truth. No faithful servant of the Lord should seek an easy or convenient way. God's vindication is far more important than man's face. Although Moses and Aaron did have some excuses, they neither argued nor pled for themselves. Many times in the past they had interceded for the people of Israel, but now they asked not for themselves. Such silence is most precious. They would rather bear the difficulty if this could give God a chance to absolve Himself.

Authority flows from ministry: it flows into people's hearts and makes them conscious of God. Ministry grows from resurrection life and is rooted in God. When a minister misrepresents God's authority his ministry ceases, just as Moses and Aaron's did. Let us therefore learn how to maintain the Lord's testimony. Let us not carelessly offer counsels, lest we fall into judgment.

May the Lord be gracious to us that we may be God-instructed. May He give grace to His church at this end-time. How we need to pray: O Lord, may Thy authority be manifested in the church; Lord, cause every brother and sister to know what authority is. The local church will be revealed when God is able to express His authority through men. Those in responsibility will not misrepresent, and the people who follow will not misunderstand. Each and every one will know his place and thus the Lord will have His way.

17 | Delegated Authorities Must Be under Authority

And it came to pass, when Saul was returned from following the Philistines, that it was told him, saying, Behold, David is in the wilderness of En-gedi. Then Saul took three thousand chosen men out of all Israel, and went to seek David and his men upon the rocks of the wild goats. And he came to the sheepcotes by the way, where was a cave; and Saul went in to cover his feet. Now David and his men were abiding in the innermost parts of the cave. And the men of David said unto him, Behold, the day of which Jehovah said unto thee, Behold, I will deliver thine enemy into thy hand, and thou shalt do to him as it shall seem good unto thee. Then David arose, and cut off the skirt of Saul's robe privily. And it came to pass afterward, that David's heart smote him, because he had cut off Saul's skirt. And he said unto his men, Jehovah forbid that I should do this thing unto my lord, Jehovah's anointed, to put forth my hand against him, seeing he is Jehovah's anointed. (1 Sam. 24.1-6)

So David and Abishai came to the people by night: and, behold, Saul lay sleeping within the place of the wagons, with his spear stuck in the ground at his head; and Abner and the people lay round about him. Then said Abishai to David, God hath delivered up thine enemy into thy hand this day: now therefore let me smite him, I pray thee, with the spear to the earth at one stroke, and I will not smite him the second time. And David said to Abishai, Destroy him not; for who can put forth his hand against Jehovah's anointed, and be guiltless? And David said, As Jehovah liveth, Jehovah will smite him; or his day shall come to die; or he shall go down into battle, and perish. Jehovah forbid that I should put forth my hand against Jehovah's anointed: but now take, I pray thee, the spear that is at his head, and the cruse of water, and let us go. So David took the spear and the cruse of water from Saul's head; and they gat them away: and no man saw it, nor knew it, neither did any awake; for they were all asleep, because a deep sleep from Jehovah was fallen upon them. (1 Sam. 26.7-12)

And David said unto the young man that told him, How knowest thou that Saul and Jonathan his son are dead? And the young man that told him said, As I happened by chance upon mount Gilboa, behold, Saul was leaning upon his spear; and, lo, the chariots and the horsemen followed hard after him. And when he looked behind him, he saw me, and called unto me. And I answered, Here am I. And he said unto me, Who art thou? And I answered him, I am an Amalekite. And he said unto me, Stand, I pray thee beside me, and slay me; for anguish hath taken hold of **me,** because my life is yet whole in me. So I stood beside him, and slew him, because I was sure that he could not live after that he was fallen: and I took the crown that was upon his head, and the bracelet that was on his arm, and have brought them hither unto my lord.

Then David took hold on his clothes, and rent them; and likewise all the men that were with him: and they mourned, and wept, and fasted until even, for Saul, and for Jonathan his son, and for the people of Jehovah, and for the house of Israel; because they were fallen by the sword. And David said unto the young man that told him, Whence art thou? And he answered, I am the son of a sojourner, an Amalekite. And David said unto him, How wast thou not afraid to put forth thy hand to destroy Jehovah's anointed? And David called one of the young men, and said, Go near, and fall upon him. And he smote him, so that he died. (2 Sam. 1.5-15)

And it came to pass after this, that David inquired of

Jehovah, saying, Shall I go up into any of the cities of Judah?
(2 Sam. 2.1)

And the sons of Rimmon the Beerothite, Rechab and
Baanah, went, and came about the heat of the day to the
house of Ish-bosheth, as he took his rest at noon. And they
came thither into the midst of the house, as though they
would have fetched wheat; and they smote him in the body:
and Rechab and Baanah his brother escaped. Now when they
came into the house, as he lay on his bed in his bedchamber,
they smote him, and slew him, and beheaded him, and took
his head, and went by the way of the Arabah all night. And
they brought the head of Ish-bosheth unto David to Hebron,
and said to the king, Behold, the head of Ish-bosheth, the son
of Saul, thine enemy, who sought thy life; and Jehovah hath
avenged my lord the king this day of Saul, and of his seed.
And David answered Rechab and Baanah his brother, the
sons of Rimmon the Beerothite, and said unto them, As
Jehovah liveth, who hath redeemed my soul out of all adver-
sity, when one told me, saying, Behold, Saul is dead, thinking
to have brought good tidings, I took hold of him, and slew
him in Ziklag, which was the reward I gave him for his
tidings. How much more, when wicked men have slain a
righteous person in his own house upon his bed, shall I not
now require his blood of your hand, and take you away from
the earth? And David commanded his young men, and they
slew them, and cut off their hands and their feet, and hanged
them up beside the pool in Hebron. But they took the head
of Ish-bosheth, and buried it in the grave of Abner in
Hebron. (2 Sam. 4.5-12)

Then came all the tribes of Israel to David unto Hebron,
and spake, saying, Behold, we are thy bone and thy flesh. In
times past, when Saul was king over us, it was thou that
leddest out and broughtest in Israel: and Jehovah said to
thee, Thou shalt be shepherd of my people Israel, and thou
shalt be prince over Israel. So all the elders of Israel came to
the king to Hebron; and king David made a covenant with

them in Hebron before Jehovah: and they anointed David king over Israel. (2 Sam. 5.1-3)

And it was so, as the ark of Jehovah came into the city of David, that Michal the daughter of Saul looked out at the window, and saw king David leaping and dancing before Jehovah; and she despised him in her heart. And they brought in the ark of Jehovah, and set it in its place, in the midst of the tent that David had pitched for it; and David offered burnt-offerings and peace-offerings before Jehovah. And when David had made an end of offering the burnt-offering and the peace-offerings, he blessed the people in the name of Jehovah of hosts. And he dealt among all the people, even among the whole multitude of Israel, both to men and women, to every one a cake of bread, and a portion of flesh, and a cake of raisins. So all the people departed every one to his house.

Then David returned to bless his household. And Michal the daughter of Saul came out to meet David, and said, How glorious was the king of Israel to-day, who uncovered himself to-day in the eyes of the handmaids of his servants, as one of the vain fellows shamelessly uncovereth himself! And David said unto Michal, It was before Jehovah, who chose me above thy father, and above all his house, to appoint me prince over the people of Jehovah, over Israel: therefore will I play before Jehovah. And I will be yet more vile than this, and will be base in mine own sight: but of the handmaids of whom thou hast spoken, of them shall I be had in honor. And Michal the daughter of Saul had no child unto the day of her death. (2 Sam. 6.16-23)

Then David the king went in, and sat before Jehovah; and he said, Who am I, O Lord Jehovah, and what is my house, that thou hast brought me thus far? (2 Sam. 7.18)

Then said the king to Ittai the Gittite, Wherefore goest thou also with us? return, and abide with the king: for thou art a foreigner, and also an exile; return to thine own place. Whereas thou camest but yesterday, should I this day make thee go up and down with us, seeing I go whither I may? return thou, and take back thy brethren; mercy and truth be with thee. (2 Sam. 15.19-20)

And, lo, Zadok also came, and all the Levites with him, bearing the ark of the covenant of God; and they set down the ark of God; and Abiathar went up, until all the people had done passing out of the city. And the king said unto Zadok, Carry back the ark of God into the city: if I shall find favor in the eyes of Jehovah, he will bring me again, and show me both it, and his habitation: but if he say thus, I have no delight in thee; behold, here am I, let him do to me as seemeth good unto him. (2 Sam. 15.24-26)

And when king David came to Bahurim, behold, there came out thence a man of the family of the house of Saul, whose name was Shimei, the son of Gera; he came out, and cursed still as he came. And he cast stones at David, and at all the servants of king David: and all the people and all the mighty men were on his right hand and on his left. And thus said Shimei when he cursed, Begone, begone, thou man of blood, and base fellow: Jehovah hath returned upon thee all the blood of the house of Saul, in whose stead thou hast reigned; and Jehovah hath delivered the kingdom into the hand of Absalom thy son; and, behold, thou art taken in thine own mischief, because thou art a man of blood.

Then said Abishai the son of Zeruiah unto the king, Why should this dead dog curse my lord the king? let me go over, I pray thee, and take off his head. And the king said, What have I to do with you, ye sons of Zeruiah? Because he curseth, and because Jehovah hath said unto him, Curse David; who then shall say, Wherefore hast thou done so? And David said to Abishai, and to all his servants, Behold, my son, who came forth from my bowels, seeketh my life: how much more may this Benjamite now do it? let him alone, and let him curse; for Jehovah hath bidden him. It may be that Jehovah will look on the wrong done unto me, and that Jehovah will requite me good for his cursing of me this day.

So David and his men went by the way; and Shimei went along on the hill-side over against him, and cursed as he went, and threw stones at him, and cast dust. And the king, and all the people that were with him, came weary; and he refreshed himself there. (2 Sam. 16.5-14)

And all the people were at strife throughout all the tribes of Israel, saying, The king delivered us out of the hand of our enemies, and he saved us out of the hand of the Philistines; and now he is fled out of the land from Absalom. And Absalom, whom we anointed over us, is dead in battle. Now therefore why speak ye not a word of bringing the king back?

And king David sent to Zadok and to Abiathar the priests, saying, Speak unto the elders of Judah, saying, Why are ye the last to bring the king back to his house? seeing the speech of all Israel is come to the king, to bring him to his house. Ye are my brethren, ye are my bone and my flesh: wherefore then are ye the last to bring back the king? And say ye to Amasa, Art thou not my bone and my flesh? God do so to me, and more also, if thou be not captain of the host before me continually in the room of Joab. And he bowed the heart of all the men of Judah, even as the heart of one man; so that they sent unto the king, saying, Return thou, and all thy servants. So the king returned, and came to the Jordan. And Judah came to Gilgal, to go to meet the king, to bring the king over the Jordan. (2 Sam. 19.9-15)

In the Old Testament time David became the second person whom God made king; the first king, Saul, had also been set up by Him. David was the authority newly raised up by God, the newly anointed of the Lord; whereas Saul was the rejected authority, the one whose anointing was in the past, for the Spirit of God had already left him. Let us now observe how David was subject to authority, making no attempt to establish his own authority.

Waiting for God to Secure Authority

1 Samuel 24 sets down what occurred in Engedi. David cut off Saul's skirt, and his heart smote him because his conscience was extremely sensitive. Chapter 26 tells how David took Saul's spear and jar of water away. He probably thought that by taking these things belonging to Saul it would be proof of his presence and he would thus be better listened to. This, however, is the way of an attorney and not the way of a Christian. A Christian is concerned with feeling, not reasoning; he deals with fact, not with evidence. Now it is true that David at the first acted like an attorney, but having the feeling of a Christian his heart could immediately be smitten. Before God we are people who care for fact and not for politics, therefore we do not emphasize procedure. Though the cutting of a skirt and the taking of a spear and water jar would make us better listened to, nevertheless our heart would still smite us.

David was one who was able to be subject to authority. He never annulled Saul's authority; he simply waited for God to secure his authority. He would not try to help God to do it; he instead would willingly wait for God. Whoever is to be God's delegated authority must learn not to try to secure authority for himself.

Authorities Must Be Both God's Choice and Church's Choice

The first chapter of 2 Samuel relates how a man slew Saul, but David then turned and judged the killer. Why? Because the slayer had violated authority. Although the violation was not directed against David, he nonetheless judged the matter because it was a violation of authority.

After Saul's death David inquired of God as to what city he should go to. Humanly speaking, David with his army should quickly descend on Jerusalem, for there was the palace. This was a chance not to be missed. Yet he asked God and God told him to go to Hebron. Hebron was only a small and insignificant city. David's going there proved that he was not trying to snatch authority on his own initiative. He waited to be anointed by the people of God. Samuel had first anointed him because he was chosen by God. Now Judah anointed him, because he was the people's choice. This action typifies the church making its choices. David could neither oppose nor refuse the people from anointing him; he could not say, "Since I already have the anointing of God upon me, I do not need your anointing." To be anointed by God is one thing; to be anointed by His people is another thing. There must be both the church's choice and God's choice. No one can force himself upon others.

David did not go up to Jerusalem, because he was waiting for God's people to anoint him. He remained in Hebron for seven years. Though it was not a short period, David was not impatient. God never chooses anyone to be an authority who is full of self and seeks for self-glory. God had anointed David to be king over the whole nation of Israel as well as over Judah, but the people of God had not yet fully accepted this. Since the house of Judah anointed him, he became king over that house first. For the rest, he was not anxious; he could wait.

After having reigned over Judah in Hebron for seven years, all the tribes of Israel anointed David as king; thus he was king in Jerusalem for thirty-three years. By its nature authority can neither be self-instigated nor imposed on others; it must be both the establishing by God and the anointing by men. To be in authority over God's children, both the anointing of the Lord and the anointing of the people are needed. Never during those seven years from age thirty to thirty-seven did David doubt that he would be anointed by the people of Israel. In this matter he submitted to the hand of God.

All those who know God can wait. If one's condition is right he will be recognized not only by the Lord as His representative but also by the church as God's representative. Let us never strive with the flesh, not even so much as to lift a finger. No one may rise up and claim, "I am God's established authority, you must

all submit to me." We must first learn to have spiritual ministry
before the Lord and then at God's time we may enter into the
midst of His children to serve them.

Maintaining Authority

Why did David have to wait at Hebron? Because after the
death of Saul, his son Ishbosheth succeeded him as king in
Jerusalem. Later on Rechab and Baanah murdered Ishbosheth
and brought his head to Hebron, thinking they were bringing
good news. Instead, David had them killed. David judged them
because they had rebelled against authority. The more one knows
how to be an authority, the more capable he is to maintain
authority. No one should ever permit another person's authority
to be damaged in order to establish his own. Whenever there is
rebellion against authority—and even if it is not directed against
you—it must be judged. Do not deal with people only when they
infringe on your authority.

No Authority before God

2 Samuel 6 tells how, when he was already king over all
Israel, David danced before the ark. Michal his wife, the daughter
of Saul, saw it and despised him in her heart. Michal thought
that, being king, he ought to be sanctified before the people of
Israel; that is, he should maintain his dignity just as her father
Saul had done. David saw it differently. He felt that in the
presence of God he had no authority whatsoever, for he was base
and contemptible. In her thinking Michal committed the same
fault as her father who, even after God had rejected him because
he had rebelled in sparing the best of the cattle and the sheep,
still wished to save his face by asking Samuel to honor him
before the people of Israel. Michal was familiar with this way of
doing things but it was different from what David knew. The

result was that God accepted David, but judged Michal by shutting up her womb. Even till now all who walk in the way of Michal will be deprived of offspring.

Anyone who represents authority should be low and humble before God and before His people. He should not be high-minded; neither should he seek to maintain his own authority among men. Though David was king on the throne, before the ark of God he was the same as his people. Michal thought David was also king in God's presence. She could not bear the sight of David dancing before the ark, hence she mocked David, saying, "How the king of Israel honors himself today!" Though some may be chosen to be in authority in the church, everyone is the same before God. Herein lies the ground and secret of authority

No Self-Consciousness of Authority

I especially like the word in 2 Samuel 7.18—"Then David the king went in, and sat before Jehovah." The temple was still to be built, therefore the ark was in a tent; and David sat on the ground. There God made a covenant with David, and there David offered an excellent prayer. In this prayer we meet a tender sensitive spirit. Before he became king, David was a mighty warrior; none could stand before him. Now that he was king, he sat humbly on the ground. He remained a humble man.

Michal, who had been born in the palace, desired to retain her majesty, just like her father. She could not see the difference between man going into God's presence and coming out from His presence. Coming out is to speak and act for God with authority, but going in is to prostrate oneself at the feet of the Lord, acknowledging what an unworthy man one is. David was truly a king set up by God, for he had the authority of God. Christ was not only son of Abraham but son of David as well. The name of the last king mentioned in all the Bible is the name of David. Then is it not surprising that David, king though he was, was not at all conscious of his kingship, only conscious of his unworthiness?

No, whoever thinks or feels that he is an authority is not worthy to be that authority. The more authority one possesses, the less that one is conscious of it. One who represents God's authority must have this blessed foolishness in him: to have authority yet to be unconscious of being an authority.

Authority Need Not Be Self-Supported

Absalom's rebellion was a double one: as a son he rebelled against his father, and as a citizen he revolted against his sovereign. When David fled the city he was in dire need of followers. Even so, he could say to Ittai, "Return, and abide with the king: for thou art a foreigner, and also an exile; return to thine own place" (2 Sam. 15.19). How tender was the heart of David. Even in his distress he would not take men away with him. To really know a person in the palace is not easy, but in trial he is clearly revealed.

Then the priests came with the ark. Now were the ark to go with David, many of the people of Israel would surely have followed. But David rose above his affliction. He would not let the ark follow him; he would rather let God do to him what He deemed good. His attitude was one of absolute subjection under the mighty hand of God. He said, "If I shall find favor in the eyes of Jehovah, he will bring me again, and show me both it, and his habitation: but if he say thus, I have no delight in thee; behold, here am I, let him do to me as seemeth good unto him" (2 Sam. 15.25-26). He persuaded Zadok and all the priests who bore the ark to go back.

Such words sound easy to say, but at a time of retreat they are exceedingly difficult to utter. Those who fled the city were few in number, and Jerusalem was full of rebellious people. David nonetheless could send his good friends back. How pure was David's heart! He went up the ascent of the Mount of Olives, weeping as he went, barefoot and with his head covered. How meek and lowly he was!

Such, indeed, is the condition of God established authority. Why strive with men? Whether or not one is king is decided by God; it does not depend on the crowds of followers, nor even on the presence of the ark. David felt no need to try to support his authority.

Authority Can Endure Provocation

A rebellious spirit is contagious. On the way, out came Shimei who cursed David continually and threw stones at him accusingly saying, "Jehovah hath returned upon thee all the blood of the house of Saul" (2 Sam. 16.8). Nothing could be further from the fact, since David had not shed any blood of the house of Saul. Nevertheless David neither argued nor sought revenge nor resisted. He still had his mighty men at his side, and it was within his power to slay that man. But he stopped them from killing Shimei, saying, "Let him alone, and let him curse; for Jehovah hath bidden him" (2 Sam. 16.11).

What a broken and tender man was David. In reading the Bible we need to touch the spirit of David at this hour. As desperate and lonely as he was at that time, surely he could at least let out some of his steam on Shimei. But David was a man of absolute obedience. He submitted to God and accepted everything as coming from God.

Let all brothers and sisters learn this lesson: the man of authority whom God establishes is able to endure provocation. If the authority you possess cannot be offended you are qualified to be in authority. Do not imagine that you can freely exercise authority because you have been appointed by God. Only the obedient are fit to be in authority.

Learn to Humble Oneself under Mighty Hand of God

David did not return to the palace immediately after the

death of Absalom. Why? Because Absalom had also been anointed as king by the people. David must therefore wait. Then the eleven tribes came to the king to ask him to return, but the tribe of Judah remained silent. So David, in order to restore their hearts, sent a message to Judah because he himself was of that tribe, though now driven out by them. He must wait for all his people to ask him back. True, David was originally set up by God; nevertheless, when trials came he learned to humble himself under the mighty hand of God. He was not anxious, nor did he fight for himself. All his battles were fought for the people of God.

All who are used by God to be in authority must have the spirit of David. Let no one defend himself nor speak for himself. Learn to wait and to be humble before God. He who knows how to obey best is he who is best qualified to be in authority. The lower one prostrates himself before God the quicker the Lord will vindicate him.

18 | The Daily Life and
Inward Motivation of Delegated Authorities

And there come near unto him James and John, the sons of Zebedee, saying unto him, Teacher, we would that thou shouldest do for us whatsoever we shall ask of thee. And he said unto them, What would ye that I should do for you? And they said unto him, Grant unto us that we may sit, one on thy right hand, and one on thy left hand, in thy glory. But Jesus said unto them, Ye know not what ye ask, Are ye able to drink the cup that I drink? or to be baptized with the baptism that I am baptized with? And they said unto him, We are able. And Jesus said unto them, The cup that I drink ye shall drink; and with the baptism that I am baptized withal shall ye be baptized; but to sit on my right hand or on my left hand is not mine to give, but it is for them for whom it hath been prepared. And when the ten heard it, they began to be moved with indignation concerning James and John. And Jesus called them to him, and saith unto them, Ye know that they who are accounted to rule over the Gentiles lord it over them; and their great ones exercise authority over them. But it is not so among you: but whosoever would become great among you, shall be your minister; and whosoever would be first among you, shall be servant of all. For the Son of man also came not to be ministered unto, but to minister, and to give his life a ransom for many. (Mark 10.35-45)

Drink the Lord's Cup and Be Baptized with the Lord's Baptism

While on earth our Lord rarely taught people how to be in

authority, for this was not His purpose in coming to the world. The clearest passage in which the Lord did instruct on authority is this one found in Mark 10. If anyone wishes to know how to be in authority he ought to read this passage. The Lord shows us here the way to authority. It all began with James and John. They longed to sit on the two sides of the Lord in His glory. Knowing the inappropriateness of such a request, they dared not come out with it directly but subtly suggested that the Lord grant them anything they might request. They wished to first obtain a promise from the Lord.

But the Lord did not quickly comply; instead, He asked what they wanted Him to do for them. So they said, "Grant unto us that we may sit, one on thy right hand, and one on thy left, in thy glory." Such a request carried two meanings: one, to be near to the Lord; two, to have more authority. It was right for them to desire nearness to the Lord, but their request went far beyond that in their desire for more authority in glory than the other ten disciples. How did the Lord answer them? As He had earlier wondered what they wanted Him to do, now He says that they themselves do not know for what they are asking.

The Lord did not reject the desire to be near Him or to be in a position of authority, nor did He find fault with the longing to sit at His right hand and left. He simply answered that they must drink His cup and be baptized with His baptism before they could sit at His right or left. James and John thought they could get what they wanted just by asking, yet the Lord replied that it was not for the asking but for drinking the cup and receiving the baptism. It is therefore evident that except men drink the Lord's cup and receive the Lord's baptism they can neither get near to the Lord nor possess authority.

What Are the Lord's Cup and Baptism?

What is the meaning of the Lord's cup? In the Garden of Gethsemane a cup was placed before the Lord, and He prayed:

"My Father, if it be possible, let this cup pass away from me: nevertheless, not as I will, but as thou wilt" (Matt. 26.39). At that moment the cup and God's will were not yet one. The cup could be removed, but the will could not be changed. The Lord might still not need to drink the cup, though desiring absolutely to do God's will. His attitude was, that if it were the will of God for Him to drink then He would drink it; but if it were not God's will, He would not drink the cup. Such words draw out our worship. What He stressed in the garden was whether or not the cup was God's will. After praying thus three times He knew that the cup and God's will were one. Hence He quickly said, "The cup which the Father hath given me, shall I not drink it?" (John 18.11) In the garden there was still the possibility of the cup passing from Him because the cup and God's will had yet to become one. After this experience in the garden, though, the Lord knew the cup was one with God's will. Therefore, outside the garden, the cup was already one with God's will. It was a cup given by the Father which He must drink.

This is a very deep spiritual lesson. The Lord was not primarily concerned with the cross; He was occupied instead with doing God's will. Although His crucifixion was trememdously important, it still could not substitute for God's will. The cross on which He died as a ransom for many may not exceed God's will. He does not come to be crucified but to do the will of God. God's will is higher than the cross. Hence the Lord's crucifixion is not because of the cross but because of doing God's will. For the sake of the Father He was crucified on the cross. He had no direct relationship with the cross; He was only directly related to God's will. His choice was God's will, not the cross. Accordingly, His drinking the cup meant His subjection to the mighty authority of God in obeying the Latter's will. And so He asked of James and John, "Are ye able to drink the cup that I drink?"

Many are able to be related to consecration or to suffering or to work, but we should maintain direct relationship only with God's will. Some people when engaged in work are not good for anything else. They become so attached to the work that they

are drowned in it. They can no longer accept any further will of
God. They insist on carrying on to the end, since they are not
working on account of God's will but for the sake of the work.
Not so with the Lord. He was so intent on doing God's will that
it was possible to Him *not* to be crucified on the cross. However,
once He became clear that God's will for Him *was* the cross, He
immediately accepted it, disregarding its unspeakable pains.
Hence His question to James and John was: Are you able to yield
to God as I yield? This is the Lord's cup.

Those who are obedient to God are connected only to God's
will; everything else is subject to change. Before doing the will of
God they must first be subject to God's authority. In the Garden
of Gethsemane the Lord reaches the peak of His obedience. He
does not mix up the cup with God's will. His object of obedience
is the will of God; the cup is not His objective. He is forever
obedient to God's will because this He considers to be higher
than all. It is neither work nor suffering nor even the cross, but
the will of God. The Lord seemed to say to James and John:
whether or not you may sit at My right hand and on My left
depends on your drinking My cup, which in this case is absolute
obedience to the will of God.

What, then, is the meaning of the Lord's baptism? This does
not refer to the baptism in the River Jordan since that was a
bygone event. No, it points to the future, to His death on the
cross. "I have a baptism to be baptized with," said the Lord,
"and how am I straitened till it be accomplished!" (Luke 12.50)
He was anticipating a release of Himself. The fulness of the glory
of God was bound up in His incarnate body. How tight, how
straitened He was! What blessing if He could be released! The
cross is therefore the release of life as well as the atonement for
sin. God releases His life through the cross.

As soon as God's life is released it will be kindled as is a fire
which is cast on earth. It will cause division instead of peace.
Whatever the fire touches it burns. Households will be divided; the
believing and the unbelieving will be in conflict; those with life and
those without life will strive against each other; and the burnt and

the unburnt will clash. This is called the Lord's baptism. Where life is, there is strife, not peace. Those who have received this baptism are separated from those who do not have it.

Hence the Lord seems to be saying here: I go to the cross to release life so that people may strive with each other; are you able to do the same thing? The baptism itself is first death and then life released; with the consequence of baptism being, to divide people. This is similar to the statement of Paul's which says that "death worketh in us, but life in you" (2 Cor. 4.12). In baptism the Lord sheds His outer shell by death and so releases life.

We ought to do the same today. We must have the outward man broken that the inner life may flow out. When a man's outer shell is broken he is brought very near to others and life may easily flow forth. Otherwise the life will remain enclosed, the spirit hard to come out, and thus the way to give life to others blocked. It is when the grain of wheat falls into the ground and has its shell burst that life begins to flow. Hence the Lord says, "Whosoever shall lose his life for my sake shall find it" (Matt. 16.25).

The Lord does not say "to die" but "to be baptized"—lest anyone should misconstrue it to mean that James and John shared in the atonement. In the matter of atonement Christ as our great high priest alone atones for our sins. There is no one else who can atone or have any part in the atonement. As regards the atoning part of His death on the cross, we have no part in it; but as to the life-releasing part of His death, we all share in it. Consequently, the Lord speaks here only of the life-releasing part of death, not of anything having to do with atonement.

Thus He appears to be saying to us: "The baptism which I will receive will break open my outer shell and release life. Are you willing to be so baptized?" Unless a man is broken, life cannot be released. An unbroken man maintains a great distance between himself and others. Though he may sit very close to people he can never touch them, because his inner life is not able to flow freely.

As soon as this life flows, the earth loses its peace and is at strife. Many shall be divided because of those with this life flowing. The difference between those who belong to the Lord and those who do not belong is great. Many difficulties will arise between those who have the Lord and those who have not, those who know God and those who do not, those who pay the price and those who do not, those who are faithful and those who are unfaithful, those who accept trials and those who refuse trials. The Lord was seemingly inferring to James and John as follows: "Since you ask to be different from the rest by sitting on My right and left, are you able today to be distinct from the rest of God's children? You first must drink the cup and be baptized with the baptism before you can sit at My right and left in glory." James and John answered presumptuously, "We are able!"

Even so, the Lord did not thereby promise them the coveted seats on His two sides. Though they might request inaccurately, the Lord had to reply correctly. His thought is: except a man drink His cup and be baptized with His baptism, he cannot sit by His right or left; and even if he does drink and is baptized, he may not sit at His side, since those places are for those for whom they have been prepared by God.

Authority Is Not Lording Over but Humbly Serving

The Lord continued His teaching on the matter of authority. He called His disciples together and instructed them about future things in glory. He said that, among the Gentiles, men seek for authority in order that they may rule over others. It is good for us to seek for the future glory, but we ought not have the thought of ruling or lording it over God's children. To do so would cause us to fall into the state of the Gentiles. To exercise authority and to rule are the desires of the Gentiles. Such a spirit must be driven from the church. Those whom the Lord uses are the ones who know the Lord's cup and the Lord's baptism. As we drink the cup and receive the baptism we will naturally have authority. It is a most ugly thing if we seek to rule over men externally. We must drive this spirit of the Gentiles out from us. Else we are unfit to lead others.

Those who seek to exercise authority should not be given authority, for God never gives authority to such persons. The more the spirit of the Gentiles dominates a person the less God can use him. But strange to say, he who senses his incompetency is the one to whom God gives authority. This is the way of the Lord and this should be our way. We should never be like politicians engaging in the political art of diplomacy. We ought not give a position to anyone out of fear that he might otherwise rebel. The way in the house of God must be spiritual and not political. Though our attitude should be gentle and soft, we must be faithful before God. A man needs to fall before God before he can be used; whenever he lifts himself up he is rejected by God.

How vastly different is authority among the Gentiles from that in the church! The first rule by position, but the second rules by the ministry of spiritual life. It is utterly ruinous for the church to fall into the state of the Gentiles. She must maintain a strict separation from them. If anyone among us reckons himself qualified to be an authority, he is most unqualified to be such. We must maintain this sensitivity in our midst.

To Be Great, One Must Be a Servant

The authority whom God appoints must have a spiritual background—he must drink the cup, that is, absolutely obey God's will; and he must receive the baptism, that is, accept death in order to release life. He must also not have any intention of exercising authority; on the contrary, he must be prepared to serve as the servant and slave of all. In other words, he possesses spiritual ground on the one hand and the spirit of humility on the other. Because he does not seek to be authority God can use him as one. It is irrelevant to talk about authority if the cup is not drunk and the baptism not received. To one who is truly humble and considers himself unfit for anything except to be servant of all, to that one the Lord announces that he may be great.

The condition for authority is consequently a sense of incompetency and unworthiness. From the Bible we can conclude that God has never used a proud soul. The moment a person becomes proud, at that moment he is laid aside by God. His hidden pride sooner or later will be revealed through his words, for words do not cease to leak out. At the future judgment seat of God even the humble will be greatly surprised. And if that be true, how much more shall be the horror of the proud on that day! We must sense our incompetency, because God only uses the useless. Polite diplomacy is not the thing here; rather is it having a sincere sense that we are but unprofitable servants. Though we have tended the flock and tilled the field, yet in coming back we still acknowledge ourselves as unprofitable servants. We do not forget to stand on the ground of a servant. God never entrusts His authority to the self-righteous and the self-competent. Let us reject pride, learn to be humble and gentle, and never speak for ourselves. Let us learn to know ourselves in the light of God.

Finally, the Lord said, "For the Son of man also came not to be ministered unto, but to minister, and to give his life a ransom for many." The Lord does not come to be authority; He comes to serve. The less one is self-conceited and the more he is humbled the more useful he will be. The more self-important and self-discriminating one is, the less is he useful. Our Lord takes the form of a slave, being born in the likeness of men. He never stretches out His hand to grasp authority, for it is given to Him by God. The Lord Jesus was exalted from humbleness to the highest; this is His life principle. Let us not stretch forth our carnal hands to grasp fleshly authority. Let us be slaves of all until one day God entrusts us with a particular responsibility. Thus shall we learn to represent God. Hence ministry is the basis of authority. Ministry comes from resurrection, service comes from ministry, and authority from service. May the Lord deliver us from high-mindedness.

How serious will be the judgment upon those who grab God's authority with their carnal hands. May we fear authority as we fear the fire of hell. To represent God is not an easy thing; it is too great and too marvelous for us to touch. We need to walk strictly in the way of obedience. The path for us is obedience, not authority; it is to be servants, not to be heads; to be slaves, not to be rulers. Both Moses and David were the greatest of authorities, yet they were not people who tried to establish their own authority. Those today who desire to be in authority ought to follow their footsteps. There should always be fear and trembling in this matter of being authority.

19 | Delegated Authorities Must Sanctify Themselves

For their sakes I sanctify myself, that they themselves
also may be sanctified in truth.   (John 17.19)

We have already seen that spiritual authority is based on spirituality. It is not something apportioned by men nor simply appointed by God. We need to remember that it is on the one hand based upon spirituality and on the other hand based upon the humble and obedient condition of the man before God. We will now add one more point, which is, that one who is to be in authority must be sanctified from the crowd. Although our Lord was sent of God and had uninterrupted communion with God, he still declared, "For their (disciples') sakes, I sanctify myself."

What Does "the Lord Sanctifying Himself" Mean?

"The Lord sanctifying Himself" means that for the sake of His disciples the Lord refrained from doing many things which were perfectly legitimate to Him, from speaking many words which He might have lawfully spoken, from maintaining many attitudes which He could have justifiably had, from putting on many kinds of apparel which would have been proper for Him, and from taking many foods which would have been normal to Him. Being the Son of God who knew no sin, His freedom far exceeded any we have on earth. Many things we cannot do because we have defects in us; many words we cannot speak for we are unclean people. But there was no such difficulty in the life of our Lord, since He is most holy. We need to humble ourselves, for our nature is full of pride. But our Lord was never proud, hence He did not need humility. Moreover, we need patience, for we are naturally impatient; our Lord, however, was never impatient, so He had no need of patience. He did not need to be restrained in many things since He was absolutely sinless. Even His anger was without sin. Nonetheless He says, "For their sakes, I sanctify myself." He was willing to be restrained in many things.

With regard to the matter of holiness, the Lord has not only His own holiness in view but ours as well. Whatever holiness we have causes us to be sanctified from the world; consequently there are many things we cannot do. Aside from His own holiness, He adds on ours, hence He sanctifies Himself. For our sake, He accepts the restrictions which come from men. Since He speaks and acts according to His holiness whereas men always speak or judge according to their sins, He was willing to accept restraint lest He be misunderstood by the sinful thoughts of men. We act not, because of sin; but He puts Himself under restraint due to holiness. We do not, for we should not; yet He does not do that which He could do. For the sake of God's authority He refrains from doing many things in order to manifest His separation from the world. This is what is meant by the Lord sanctifying Himself.

To Be in Authority Often Means Loneliness

In learning to be in authority we ought to be sanctified before brothers and sisters. Many legitimate things we cannot do and many lawful words we cannot speak. We must be sanctified both in words and in sentiments. According to ourselves we take a certain attitude, but among God's children we will be sanctified. Even our fellowship with brothers and sisters must have a limit beyond which we will neither be casual nor frivolous. We should rather lose our liberty, we rather will be lonely. Loneliness is the mark of authority. It is not due to pride but for the sake of representing God's authority.

There is not a question of sin here, only a matter of sanctification. The opposite of holiness is commonness, not sin. To be sanctified is to be different from others. Many rightful things we will not do, many speakable words we will not utter. This is not an outward pretension but the restraint of God in the spirit. Only in this way can we be God's delegated authorities.

One who is in authority represents God in his every word and action. As we see in Numbers 20.12 Moses failed to sanctify God in the eyes of the people of Israel and he did not sanctify himself before them. He misrepresented God, hence he could not enter Canaan. The sparrows fly in flocks, whereas the eagles fly singly. If we can only fly at a low level because we cannot bear the solitude of high flying we are unfit to be in authority. To be in authority requires restraint; one must sanctify himself. Others may, but you cannot; others may speak, but you cannot. You must obey the Spirit of the Lord as He teaches within you. You may feel lonely and miss the fervor of the crowd; nevertheless, you dare not mingle with the brothers and sisters in joking and jesting. This is the price of authority. Unless we sanctify ourselves like our Lord we are not qualified to be in authority.

Even so, as regards being members one of another, whoever is in authority should be perfectly normal in maintaining the fellowship of the body with all the brothers and sisters. Accordingly, in representing God he must sanctify himself under the restraint of God that he may be an example to all; while as a member of the body he should serve with all his brethren in coordination, never assuming the false position of being in a special class.

To Be in Authority Requires Restraining One's Affections

Leviticus 10.1-7 records the judgment of Nadab and Abihu because they failed to be subject to the authority of their father

Aaron. On the same day their father was anointed, Aaron's four sons were also anointed in the sanctuary to be priests. They were not to serve individually but to help their father in God's service. And so they were not permitted to initiate anything. Now without their father's permission and according to their own thoughts Nadab and Abihu offered strange fire; and consequently, they were consumed by fire. Then Moses said to Aaron: "This is what the Lord has said, 'I will show myself holy among those who are near me.'" In this incident God reveals something: those who are near Him should never be careless. There is a much severer discipline applied to them than to the people in general.

What could Aaron do when two of his four sons, Nadab and Abihu, died in one day? For he had a double relationship here: he was the priest before God but he was also the head of his family. Can a person serve God to the extent of forgetting his own son? According to the custom of the people of Israel, when there was a death in the family the members of the family would let their hair hang loose and rend their clothes. Yet in this instance Moses commanded that the bodies be carried out and forbade Aaron and his two remaining sons to follow the custom of the day.

Mourning is a normal human affection and is perfectly legitimate. But to those Israelites who served God, as here, it was forbidden lest they die. How serious this is. Those who served God were judged differently from the ordinary Israelites. What all other people of Israel might do, they could not. For a father to mourn for his son, for brothers to wail over brothers, was both lawful and natural; nonetheless, those who had the holy oil upon them must sanctify themselves. No question of sin on their part was involved in this case. Yet not everything which is legitimate, even though sin is not involved, can be indiscriminately done. The issue is not over sin but over sanctification.

As has already been mentioned, the opposite of holiness is commonness. Holiness means that others may, but I cannot. What the disciples may do, the Lord does not. What other brothers may do, those in authority cannot do. Even láwful affection needs to be put under control, otherwise death can be the consequence. The people of Israel died because of their sins, but priests may die because of not being sanctified. With the Israelites, he who killed must die; for Aaron, however, if he had mourned for his sons he would have died. People in authority must pay the price for it.

Aaron could not even go out of the tabernacle; he had to let others bury the dead. The people of Israel did not live in the tabernacle, whereas Aaron and his sons were not allowed to step out of the door of the tabernacle. They must diligently keep God's charge. The anointing oil sanctifies us from our natural affections as well as from customary conduct. We should respect the anointing oil which God gives to us.

Let us therefore have a thorough dealing before God with respect to our being sanctified from the rest of the people. The world and ordinary brothers and sisters may continue their family affections, but God's delegated authorities must maintain the glory of God. They ought not set loose their own affections and act carelessly or rebelliously; rather, they must praise the Lord for seeing His glory.

Those who serve are anointed by God. They should sacrifice their own affections, denying even legitimate ones. All who would maintain God's authority must know how to oppose their own feelings, how to lay aside the deepest of their affections towards their relatives, friends and loved ones. The demand of God is exacting: unless one lays aside his own affections he cannot serve God. He who is sanctified is God's servant; he who is not sanctified is a common person.

Sanctified in Life and Enjoyment

Why did Nadab and Abihu offer strange fire? We read that after what had happened to them God told Aaron, "Drink no wine nor strong drink, thou, nor thy sons with thee, when ye go into the tent of meeting" (Lev. 10.9). All who know how to read the Bible agree that these two men offered strange fire because they were drunk. The people of Israel were allowed to drink wine and strong drink, but the priests of God were absolutely forbidden to touch them.

It is therefore a matter of enjoyment. Others may enjoy, but we cannot. Others may rejoice in pleasures (for wine speaks of rejoicing), but we cannot. People serving God are under discipline that they may be able to distinguish between the holy and the common, and between the unclean and the clean. Though we do indeed need to maintain the fellowship of the body with all brothers and sisters, nevertheless in times of special service we should not be careless. Whatever loosens the reins of restraint is not to be done.

Leviticus 21 records the special demands God made on the priests who served Him to sanctify themselves. These demands were the following:

1. Not one of them should defile himself for the dead among his people, except for his nearest of kin. (This was an ordinary request.)

2 They must be sanctified in clothing and in body. They should not make tonsures upon their heads, nor shave off the edges of their beards (since these were done by the Egyptians in worshiping the sun), nor make any cuttings in their flesh (this was done by the Africans).

3. They must be sanctified in marriage.

4. As to the high priest, the demands of God were even more exacting. He should not go in to any dead body, nor should the high priest defile himself even for his father or for his mother.

The higher the office, the stricter the demand. The degree of nearness to God becomes the degree of His demand. Of him to whom God entrusts more, the more will He demand. God is especially concerned with whether or not His servants have sanctified themselves.

Authority Is Based on Sanctification

Authority has its foundation in sanctification. Without sanctification there can be no authority. If you wish to live with the crowd you cannot be an authority. You cannot represent God if you maintain a very liberal and loose communication with the people. The higher the authority the greater the separation. God is the highest authority; consequently He is above all. Let us learn to be sanctified from things unclean or common. The Lord Jesus may do whatsoever He likes, but for the sake of His disciples He sanctifies Himself. He steps aside and stands on the side of holiness.

May we heartily desire to please God too and thus seek after deeper sanctification. It means we will be distinguished from the common, although not separated from God's children as though we were holier than they. The more we are sanctified and are subject to the authority of God the more we may be delegated authorities. If those in authority in the church fail, how can obedience be maintained? Unless this matter of authority is solved the church will always be chaotic.

He who is in authority does not grasp authority; he serves God, is willing to pay the price, and seeks not excitement. To be in authority requires one to climb high, to not fear loneliness, and to be sanctified. May we be those who lay our all on the altar so that God's authority may be restored. This is the way of the Lord in His church.

The Conditions for Being Delegated Authorities

Wives, be in subjection unto your own husbands, as unto the Lord . . .Husbands, love your wives, even as Christ also loved the church, and gave himself up for it . . . Even so ought husbands also to love their own wives as their own bodies. He that loveth his own wife loveth himself . . . Nevertheless do ye also severally love each one his own wife even as himself; and let the wife see that she fear her husband. (Eph. 5.22,25,28,33)

Children, obey your parents in the Lord: for this is right . . . And, ye fathers, provoke not your children to wrath; but nuture them in the chastening and admonition of the Lord . . . And, ye masters, do the same things unto them, and forbear threatening: knowing that he who is both their Master and yours is in heaven, and there is no respect of persons with him. (Eph. 6.1,4,9)

God standeth in the congregation of God; He judgeth among the gods. How long will ye judge unjustly, and respect the persons of the wicked? (Ps. 82.1-2)

If any man is blameless, the husband of one wife, having children that believe, who are not accused of riot or unruly. For the bishop must be blameless, as God's steward; not self-willed, not soon angry, no brawler, no striker, not greedy of filthy lucre; but given to hospitality, a lover of good, sober-minded, just, holy, self-controlled. (Titus 1.6-8)

One that ruleth well his own house, having his children in subjection with all gravity; (but if a man knoweth not how to rule his own house, how shall he take care of the church of God?) not a novice, lest being puffed up he fall into the condemnation of the devil. (1 Tim. 3.4-6)

These things speak and exhort and reprove with all authority. Let no man despise thee. (Titus 2.15)

Let no man despise thy youth; but be thou an ensample to them that believe, in word, in manner of life, in love, in faith, in purity. (1 Tim. 4.12)

For hereunto were ye called: because Christ also suffered for you, leaving you an example, that ye should follow his steps. (1 Peter 2.21)

The authorities whom God has established in the family are the parents in relation to their children, the husbands in relation to their wives, and the masters in relation to their servants. In the world the authorities are the kings in relation to their subjects and the rulers in relation to their subordinates. In the church it is the elders in relation to God's people and the workers in relation to their work. All these various authoritie have their respective conditions.

1. *Husbands.* The Bible teaches that wives should be subject to their husbands; yet husbands should exercise authority with a condition. Three times in Ephesians 5 are husbands called upon to love their wives even as they love themselves. Undoubtedly there is authority in the family; nonetheless those in authority need to fulfill God's requirement. The love of Christ for the church sets the example for the love which husbands ought to give their own wives. As Christ loves the church so should husbands love their wives. The love of the husbands ought to be the same as the love of Christ for His church. If husbands wish to represent God's authority they must love their own wives.

2. *Parents.* Unquestionably children must obey their parents; even so, the authority of the parents has its responsibility and condition too. The scripture says, "Fathers, provoke not your children to wrath." In spite of the fact that parents do have

authority, they need to learn how to control themselves before God. They should not deal with their children according to their whims, thinking that they have the absolute right to do so since they have begotten and do rear them. Even though God created us, He has never ill-treated us. It is not right to do to children what one would usually dare not do to friends, students, subordinates, or relatives.

A paramount need for parents is to control themselves, that is, to be able to control themselves by the Holy Spirit. There is a limit to what parents can do to their children. The objective of all the authority parents have towards their children is to instruct, to bring their children up in the discipline and admonition of the Lord. No thought of overlording or punishing is involved; the intention is for education and loving protection.

3. *Masters.* The servants ought to be obedient to their masters, yet to be a master is likewise conditional. Masters should not threaten or provoke their servants. God will not allow His delegated authorities to act intemperately; they must have the fear of God within them. They need to know that He who is both their Master and their servants' Master is in heaven and that there is no partiality with Him (Eph. 6.9). Remember well that masters also are under authority. Although people are under their authority, they themselves are under authority—the authority of God. For this reason they cannot be unbridled. The more a person knows about authority the less arrogant and intimidating he becomes. The indispensable attitudes of those in authority are gentleness and love. If one menaces and judges others he himself will soon be judged by God. Therefore masters ought to tremble before God.

4. *Rulers.* We should be subject to the governing authorities. Nowhere in all the New Testament is there any instruction on how to be a ruler. Can this be a hint that God has given the world to the non-believers to rule rather than to the Christians? According to the New Testament, it would appear God does not

intend that Christians in this age be rulers on the earth. However, the Old Testament does describe to us the conditions of rulers. The basic requirements for governing authorities are righteousness, impartiality, justice, and care for the poor. These are the principles which rulers must keep. They are not out to support themselves but to maintain absolute justice.

5. *Elders.* The elders are the authorities in the local assembly. The brethren should learn to be subject to the elders. One essential quality of elders, as enumerated in Titus 1, is self-control. The lawless can never enforce the law; neither can the rebellious bring in submission. The elders must first be strictly self-controlled. How prevalent among men is the phenomenon of a lack of restraint; consequently in appointing elders let it be the specially disciplined who are chosen. Since the elders are set up in order to take care of the church, they themselves must first know how to obey and be under control that they may be examples to all others. God never appoints to be an elder anyone who likes to put himself first (such as Diotrephes, 3 John 9). Being the highest authority in the local assembly, elders must be self-controlled persons.

In 1 Timothy 3 and 4 another essential quality of an elder is mentioned: he must manage his own household well. This household refers not primarily to parents or wives but especially to the children. The children must be kept submissive and respectful in every way. He who knows how to be a good father may be chosen an elder. Exercising proper authority at home, he is qualified to be an elder in the church.

An elder must not be a self-conceited person. He who becomes haughty when given authority is unfit for the elderhood. The elders of a local assembly should not be susceptible to power consciousness. Whoever is conscious of authority is not fit to be an elder, nor can he manage the affairs of the church. Only small people are proud; they cannot bear either God's glory or His trust and use of them. Hence, a recent convert must not be chosen as elder lest he be puffed up and fall into the condemnation of the devil. (The Greek meaning of a novice is illustrated by a carpenter's apprentice who handles an ax for the first time.)

6. *Workers.* In Titus 2.15 the condition for workers as delegated authorities in the work is specified. Titus was not an elder of the church but served the Lord on the basis of an apostle. Paul exhorted him: "These things speak and exhort and reprove with all authority. Let no man despise thee." In order not to be despised one must sanctify himself. If he is no different from others in living and conduct, if he lives loosely and without discipline, he cannot escape being despised. It takes self-discipline to draw respect from others and to qualify oneself as God's representative. Paul speaks to Timothy in the same vein. Though it is true that a worker does not seek glory and honor from men, he still cannot allow himself to be despised through his lack of sanctification.

Only two books in the entire New Testament are written to young workers. In both, Paul exhorts that they do not let themselves be despised because of their youth; on the contrary, they should set an example for the other believers. They must reject all things which might cause them to be despised. To be in authority is costly; such ones need to be sanctified from the rest and be ready for a lonely life. Those who are examples differ from the rest in having sanctified themselves. Now no one should lift himself up, yet neither should he allow himself to be despised. Never be self-conceited, but never be disregarded either. As soon as one becomes too common, he is dropped from the work. His usefulness is gone, and his authority is lost.

It is exceedingly important that God's authority be maintained. Authority is manifested in sanctification, not in commonness. To represent authority is to represent God; to be in authority is to be an example to all.

TITLES YOU
WILL WANT TO HAVE

by Watchman Nee

Basic Lesson Series
Volume 1 — A Living Sacrifice
Volume 2 — The Good Confession
Volume 3 — Assembling Together
Volume 4 — Not I, But Christ
Volume 5 — Do All to the Glory of God
Volume 6 — Love One Another

The Church and the Work
Volume 1 — Assembly Life
Volume 2 — Rethinking the Work
Volume 3 — Church Affairs

The Spirit Of Judgment
From Faith to Faith
The Lord My Portion
Aids to "Revelation"
Grace for Grace
The Better Covenant
A Balanced Christian Life
The Mystery of Creation
The Messenger of the Cross
Full of Grace and Truth — Volume 1
Full of Grace and Truth — Volume 2
The Spirit of Wisdom and Revelation
Whom Shall I Send?
The Testimony of God
The Salvation of the Soul
The King and the Kingdom of Heaven
The Body of Christ: A Reality
Let Us Pray
God's Plan and the Overcomers
The Glory of His Life
"Come, Lord Jesus"
Practical Issues of This Life
Gospel Dialogue
God's Work
Ye Search the Scriptures
The Prayer Ministry of the Church
Christ the Sum of All Spiritual Things
Spiritual Knowledge
The Latent Power of the Soul
Spiritual Authority
The Ministry of God's Word
Spiritual Reality or Obsession
The Spiritual Man

by Stephen Kaung

Discipled to Christ
The Splendor of His Ways
Seeing the Lord's End in Job
The Songs of Degrees
Meditations on Fifteen Psalms

ORDER FROM:

Christian Fellowship Publishers, Inc
11515 Allecingie Parkway
Richmond, Virginia 23235